TURKISH ST
FROM FOUR DECADES

Note on Translator

Louis Mitler

A native of Lexington, Ky., he graduated from the College of Letters (Edibiyat Fakültesi), Istanbul University, in philosophy and has lived and worked extensively in Turkey and Iran. He holds an M.A. in history and a Master of Library Science from the University of Kentucky. He worked as Turkish and Farsi Cataloger at the Library of Congress before becoming active as a translator. He is the author of two reference books, *Ottoman Turkish Writers* and *Contemporary Turkish Writers*. He currently operates a translation bureau focusing on Middle Eastern languages in Charlottesville, Va.

TURKISH STORIES FROM FOUR DECADES

by Aziz Nesin
(Mehmet Nusret Nesin)

Selected and Translated by
Louis Mitler

An Original by
Three Continents Press

Library of Congress Cataloging-in-Publication Data

Nesin, Aziz.
　[Short stories.　English.　Selections]
　Turkish stories from four decades / by Aziz Nesin : selected
and translated by Louis Mitler. -- 1st ed.
　　p.　cm.
　Includes bibliographical references.
　ISBN 0-89410-687-2 (cloth) : $24.00. -- ISBN 0-89410-688-0
(pbk.) : $13.00
　I. Mitler, Louis, 1944-　II. Title.
PL248.N43A25　1991
894' .3533--dc20　　　　　　　　　　　　　　　　91-50114
　　　　　　　　　　　　　　　　　　　　　　　　　　CIP

CONTENTS

Translator's Foreword

As translator of this volume, I had three responsibilities: the selection of which works to include, the task of turning the original text into grammatical English and the business of molding that English into a language that transmitted what I felt the atmosphere of the story to be, without changing Nesin's meaning.

The choice of what to include, and thus what to exclude, was perhaps the most difficult job. I was confronted by a huge body of as yet untranslated short stories, written in a period of over forty years, dealing with most aspects of mankind's "sorry scheme of things entire". Some were written in a simple narrative style. Some were surreal tales or abstract parables. A few, like the *Neutron Bomb*, purported to be newspaper articles. Was I to attempt to present a small cross sample of Nesin's short story authorship, choosing works on the basis of the years of their authorship and the predominant style in which they were written as well as their subject matter? Would this "laboratory" approach give an English-speaking readership a superior overview of Nesin, the short story writer, or should I simply include a random selection of works that had "rung true" for me or pleased me personally?

In the end, I sought to do a little of both by including samples from Aziz Nesin's early writings as well as from his latest works while, at the same time, I attempted to include a few examples of stories in each of his principal styles.

While the translation of the text was less problematic than the choice of material, there were quandaries. There are generally a number of "correct" ways to translate any given passage that may not convey the intended meaning. Should the translator intervene in the creation of the work to turn the grammatically "correct" English text into something that is not only understandable but persuasive and moves the reader into the emotional space that Nesin intended his Turkish readers to occupy? How do you handle dialect? Do you turn an Istanbul tough into a Cockney gangster or Chicago mafioso, something that others occasionally have done to charming but misleading effect? I have attempted to hew to a standard, American English, whether the speaker was a peasant, a sultan or a newspaper publisher to avoid creating an ambiance other than that the author had in mind.

Other limiting factors are puns and double meanings, nonsense formulas, such as are found in folk and fairy tales ("once upon a time"), and onomatopoeic phrases ("*paldır küldür*"), together with long passages of metric and/or rhyming poetry. If such passages are too long or too central to the narrative line or denouement of the story and the translator doubtful that he can preserve both form and meaning in the target language, such works are best passed over, regretfully. Thus I have had to reject several intriguing stories because they derived their central meaning from puns.

I would like to express here my appreciation for the influence of my *hojas*, Prof. Dr. Macit Gökberk and Prof. Dr. Sabri Esat Siyavuşgil, respectively chairmen of the Department of Philosophy and the Department of Psychology at the University of Istanbul, not only for their contribution to my interest in the Turkish language and literature but in Turkish culture in general.

Introduction

AZIZ NESIN
Humorist and Humanitarian

Like Aziz Nesin there are numbers of modern Turkish authors who were born into privation, have had their works censored and suffered imprisonment. Some, like poet Nazim Hikmet, passed much of their lives in exile while others were killed under unclarified circumstances, like Nesin's collaborator Sabahattin Ali. What makes Nesin's career and work distinctive among the writings and lives of these fellow writers, some of whose works are still unobtainable in their own country and almost all of whose names are unknown abroad?

To an outside observer it would almost seem that only *kismet*, that irresistible destiny in which pious Muslims believe, could have preserved Nesin alive through the prisons and banning such as eventually engulfed Kemal Tahir, Halikarnas Balıkçısı, "The Fisherman of Halicarnassus", Necib Fazıl Kısakürek and so many more. Under such repression literary voices not totally silenced turned to "safer" forms of self-expression or, like the Garipler of the 1940's, Turkish proto-Beatniks, they wrote poetry so *avant garde* and abstruse that it was ignored by the authorities. Nesin did none of these things.

Perhaps it is that very sense of *kismet*, a feeling of resignation which penetrates the popular Turkish psyche even deeper than the tenants of orthodox Islam, which differentiates Nesin's outlook in part from the sermonizing tone of many of his fellow leftist reformers whose outlooks were rooted in the West.

Nesin was early steeped not only in the popular Islamic tradition, but as he explains in his autobiographical *Böyle Gelmiş Böyle Gitmez* ("Istanbul Boy", Austin, 1977, 1979), he was exposed to story telling and narratives derived from Karagöz, the "Punch and Judy", not yet extinct in poor neighborhoods in his youth. From these derive the traditional "nonsense" formulas, the symmetrical patterns of repeated conversation and action leading to a denouement and Nesin's tendency to use archetypes representing different sorts of personalities rather than psychologically realistic characters in his stories. Other derivations from the *masallar* or Turkish folk tale are the use of the "moral" and a general atmosphere of exaggeration and hyperbolae. But perhaps his more important debt to popular tradition is a sense of the absurdity and injustice of life, coupled with an atmosphere of acceptance, an acquiescence to *kismet* that no reformer rooted in the reform-minded West, whether leftist or rightist, could consciously countenance.

But the ingenuity and tenacity with which Nesin has managed to produce his books, perform his plays and publish his articles, and heap up awards, against all odds, belie an image of resignation and passivity. By the use of fairy tales and surreal formats, by setting some stories in China (a benighted Communist land where the censors assumed anything could happen) and by writing under a number of feminine names as well as the names of his children, Nesin managed for a while to evade the censorship. Ironically, after all this subterfuge, a major prison sentence was imposed on him for his having allegedly translated a subversive article from French, a language he did not know!

After his orphanage upbringing, prison sentences and years

of penury, it might be thought that Nesin would qualify as well as any member of the Village Institute School of Turkish Social Fiction for a certificate from the "Academy of Hard Knocks". It may be partly due to his credentials from this "Academy" that Nesin writes with an empathy for the downtrodden absent in the fiction of earlier depictions of the masses in Turkish literature: the somewhat patronizing portrayals of the poor in the novels Hüseyin Rahmi Gürpınar or the melodramas of Refik Halit Karay. But it is also true that it is by his bitter-sweet, sometimes bawdy and streetwise humor and the absence of didactic formulas and ready-made "solutions" that Nesin diverges from the earnestness of contemporary leftist reformers.

It is true that Nesin's terse style, paucity of atmosphere and characterizations, although it is a minimalism unknown to Zola, de Maupassant or Gorki, owe something to Western sources.

The fact is that the orphanage that Nesin attended, the Dar üs-Şafaka, was considered one of the best high schools in Istanbul at the time Nesin attended it and his education at the Military Academy may have been sounder than that of some of his more affluent literary contemporaries. Nesin's eclectic reading in world fiction is echoed throughout his stories. For example, "The First Woman to Understand Me," replicates the line of Thomas Mann's "Little Mister Friedmann," but, unlike Mann, instead of closing with the hero's drowning himself in a brook, *The First Woman* has a cynical and earthy ending typical of the tone of the other stories. A different twist on Franz Kafka's *Metamorphoses*, *We Humans* ends with the protagonist finding enlightenment through his monster condition and his *Jesus and Two People* mercilessly lampoons the story of the Good Samaritan.

But Nesin has chosen the parable and folk-like tale ("such as La Fontaine never wrote") as his favored means of expression in preference to the realistic story in the Gorkian tradition.

In many of these stories, the theme of the scapegoat or innocent victim of a world ruled by knaves and fools is paired with the motif of the donkey, an animal indispensable to pre-mechanized agriculture but despised by men in the same degree as it is useful to them. While many of Nesin's protagonists are clown-like characters of the "He Who Gets Slapped" variety, beneath their white face paint flow the tears of the Pagliaccio. The protagonist, especially when the narrative is in the first person, tends to be a victim of life, a state of things uncommon in the fiction of the contemporary United States where a Nietzschian distaste for "losers" seems to prevail.

There are some concessions to the custom that "a humor story must have a 'happy ending'" but they are minimal compromises with convention and somehow emphasize the bite of the tale.

The author eats the sweetest baklava he has ever tasted after the bitterness of seeing his old friend's hometown desecrated (*What Happened to the Privy of the Forty Stairs?*) The Cheater is resigned to being cheated in *Don't You Have Any Donkeys in Your Country?*

On the whole Nesin's world is a rough place.

Rulers are tyrants as well as nincompoops (*The Grand Vizier's Donkey*). They are capable of destroying humanity, or that part of humanity they consider less worthy of life than themselves, without remorse, as long as they can save the buildings and "the lace curtains at the windows" (*The Neutron Bomb Will Save Civilization*). They are surrounded by servile and dishonest flatterers (*We Resemble You*). Development programs are mostly unproductive panoplies to indulge the vanity of an elite (*Clinkity Clank*). Appointments to public office are capricious (*The Reference Card*). Lower authorities are stupid and overbearing (*Hamdi the Elephant*) or arbitrary and greedy (*Madman for a Hundred Liras*).

The streets are filled with thugs, perverts and madmen (*One by One, We Fell by the Way*) and lunatics may even invade one's own home (*Does Anyone Know Pumpkin Muam-*

mer?). Humility and kindness are rewarded by abuse (*Number Fifteen*) or even violent death (*Jesus and Two People*). At the very best, everyone is on the grab and even swindlers can get swindled (*Don't You Have Any Donkeys in Your Country?)*

The rewards of a long life are to see familiar surroundings destroyed (*What Happened to the Privy of the Forty Stairs?*) and to experience rejection by self-centered friends and avaricious relatives (*How They Loved the Old Man*). When you die, your relatives merely use your funeral to display their social status or political rank (*The Made-to-order Funeral Oration*).

Women are heartless, castrating creatures (like the old sweetheart in *Bravoo*). The kindest member of their sex represented in these stories is the whore (in *The First Woman Ever to Understand Me*), unless it be the amazing young girl who gives herself totally to the old man without hope of reward other than his affection (*How They Loved the Old Man*). Doctors are either incompetent (*A Pair of Glasses*) or outright charlatans (*A Hair from a Toothbrush*). Lawyers are remorseless mercenaries (*He Earned It!*). Indeed, men are "totally depraved" in a sense that Calvin himself might endorse and they know it in their hearts (the Surgeon who bashes out the Good Samaritan's brains in *Jesus and Two People*) yet they can achieve a sort of tolerance of their fellow man if they look in the " 'I' Mirror" (*We Humans*).

While every society bears the distinctive imprint of its history and traditions, all humans are bound together in common longings and frustrations rooted in their common biological structure and the conditions of their lives. It is to these common yearnings that Nesin chiefly addresses himself and it is through these shared cravings that we see ourselves in the characters of his stories.

When I consulted the author about which stories he would recommend my turning into English, he replied, "I don't know the likes and dislikes of the American reader. You know this better than I do."

I trust that I have been able to select a sampling of stories from Nesin's prolific output so as to support the observation of Octavio Paz, who in his essay *Traducción y literalidad* (Barcelona, 1971) says, "Translation is possible because in every era and every clime, men always say the same things."

Louis Mitler
December 12, 1990

Aziz Nesin Chronology

1915-(Dec 20) Born at Heybeyliada (Khalki Island), Istanbul

1925-Started school with the third grade at the *Kanuni Sultan Süleyman* elementary school

1926-Entered Dar üs-Şafaka (City Orphanage) at the fourth grade

1937-Graduated from Military Academy, Ankara as second lieutenant

1940-Army Military Engineers Corps, first marriage

1942-Company Commander, Erzurum, Engineering Battalion. Injured in a bomb accident. Was assigned to clear the military munitions depot destroyed in the Erzincan earthquake (Dec. 27, 1939, between 23,000 and 30,000 killed)

1944-Discharged from army for having "misused his authority" and sentenced to three months ten days imprisonment

1946-Held and subjected to "severe questioning" in the State Security Offices (Sansaryan Building) for seventeen days following the great roundup of leftist suspects on Dec 16. Was sentenced to ten months by a court martial for a brochure condemning American imperialism and the exercise of the Truman doctrine in Turkey

1948-Held for two months during trial for his satirical book *Azizname*. Acquitted by the Istanbul Second Criminal Court

1949-Served six months for having "insulted Princess Elizabeth of England, the Shah of Iran and the King of Egypt's wife" in a story

1950-Published a magazine *Baştan* [From the Start]. When this was closed he started publishing another magazine called *Yeni Baştan* [New *Baştan* or "Starting All Over Again"]. He was condemned to sixteen months imprisonment and sixteen months of banning under Turkish Criminal Code para. 142 for having translated an article, which was judged objectionable from French, although he did not know the French language

1954-After release from prison and various failed business ventures, he begins to write for the humor magazine *Akbaba* [The Vulture] under over two hundred assumed names since he could not publish any longer under his own name

1955-Was arrested by Martial Law government after the September 6 and 7 anti-minority riots in Istanbul. Released after six months without even being indicted. Married Meral Çelen (having divorced first wife in 1948)

1961-Indicted for an article in the daily newspaper *Tanin*. Released after four months incarceration

1962-$320,000 worth of books burned up under mysterious circumstances in his Düşün Printing House

1965-Obtained his first passport and permission to go abroad. Visited Eastern Block countries. Won Bulgarian "Golden Hedgehog" Award for his story *Vatani Vazife* [Patriotic Duty]

1972-Founded the Nesin Trust for orphans (went into operation 1982)

1977-General Secretary of the Turkish Writers Union

1982-Returning from Asian-African Writers Meeting in Vietnam, he suffered a heart attack and was treated in Moscow for a month

1983-Invited to a conference at Indiana University but his passport was taken back and he was not allowed to attend. Suffered stroke. Helped to prepare a "Petition from the Intelligentsia"

1985-Elected member of PEN Club by West Germany and the UK

The Reference Card

("Tavsiye Kartı" from *Mahallenin Kismetı,* 1957)

I became friends on the train right away with Nafi Bey.

"Efendi, I'm going to Ankara for a reference card," he said. "If you don't mind, I will tell you all about it. Six months ago I made my first trip. There is a certain Zeki Bey, a very good person, though I don't mean to say that he is better than yourself. I all but brought him up. When he was little, the whole neighborhood used to call on Allah and his Prophet for deliverance from him. Everyone shook their collars in dismay at him. He was such a naughty, such a pestiferous brat..."

I tried not to listen to Nafi Bey but I had no choice. He kept on yakking right in my ear.

"Oh, he was so naughty. Pardon the expression, but whatever mischief you can think of, he used to do it. We used to say in the neighborhood that this boy would never in the world amount to anything. Well, Bey Effendi, the Good Lord enlightened the boy's mind so that he did become somebody and he became more of a somebody than almost anybody. When he became somebody, he left Istanbul and settled in Ankara. So, six months ago, I, your humble servant, went to see this Zeki, excuse me, Zeki Bey. I don't know why, but he couldn't seem to

11

recognize my humble self. 'Oh but Zeki Bey, didn't you used to live in Nemse Alley, next door to the Convent of the Sandalled Dervishes?' I asked him."

"'Where is this Nemse Alley supposed to be? We never lived any place other than up in Shishli. The only other place we used to go to was the Islands for our summer holidays,' he said."

"'But Bey Effendi, has your humble servant made a mistake? Is Your Excellency not the son of Policeman Tahir Bey?' I asked him."

"'What policeman?' he shouted. 'Yes, my father's name was Tahir but he wasn't a policeman, he was Chief of Secret Operations in the Bureau of Public Security."

"I then understood that Tahir Bey must have received a promotion after he had retired. No matter what I said, I couldn't get Zeki Bey to recognize me."

"Finally, I said, 'In fact, one day you slipped into our garden and climbed up our plum tree. Don't you remember?'"

"He didn't."

"'Then, I chased Your Excellency out and Your Excellency fell from the tree in fright and cut your lip on a tin pail that was sitting on the ground. There, you still have the scar,' I said."

" 'Well, anyway, what is it you want? Just tell me. Do you want a reference? It doesn't matter whether I know who you are or not,' he said."

" 'Ah, effendi, how well you have understood,' I said. He immediately pulled a card out of his wallet. and wrote on it, 'Please show all necessary *facilité* to Nafi Bey, the bearer of this card.' When I read the card, I said, 'I don't need *facilité*, I need work.' "

"'That's how it's done. That's how it's written,' he said."

"I took the card and went back to Istanbul. My dear sir, how stupid I was. I went all the way to Ankara, got the card and came back but I didn't ask who to give it to. Bey Effendi, could anybody have kept their head in a moment like that?"

"When I got home with the card, it all came to me. Who am I going to give this card to, for goodness sake? There wasn't anything on the card about giving it to this or that person or official. Do I have to go back to Ankara to ask? I said to myself that I would ask somebody who understands this sort of business but, sir, it would appear that everybody but me knew how these things were done. Getting a reference card is one thing, using it is another, Bey Effendi."

"A friend of mine said, 'Oh, Nafi Bey, don't you know anything at all? Look at the signature on the card. Some signatures work in such and such an office but some are like a "pay to the bearer" bank draft and are good for anything. Good heavens, your signature is one that's good everywhere. If you like, you can take it to the Auction Rooms in the Bazaar or the Town Hall or the Governor's Office. With the permission of Allah, that card will work anywhere.'"

"Ah, my dear Bey Effendi, I had won the lottery and hadn't known it. 'This card works all over and I should be sorry for my ingratitude', I said to myself. I went straight to the Director General's office."

"Just see if you could get in to see the Director General! It's easy to get the card, what is hard is to give the card to somebody. I wanted to leave but they said not to. Just suppose I were a civil servant. I waited from eight in the morning till eight at night at the door of the Director General. Once in a great while the Director General would appear before me like a vision. Before I could spring up, they would tell me either that he had gone out or that he was talking to the press. What 'Director General' means is that people can't see you."

"A month went by like this. One night at home, I thought about it and stuck my hand in my wallet to see how my reference card was getting along. It could happen. They could admit me into the Director General's presence and I could reach into my wallet and no card! It might happen that they had stolen it. If the Director General Bey said to say to me, 'If you don't even have a reference card, what do you mean by coming into my presence? Get out of my sight!' wouldn't he be right? I had put the card, not in my wallet but in the inner pocket of my coat, right over my heart. I had found my card but my card was ruined."

"I had sweated a lot running to and fro. The card had turned to sponge from my sweat. The reference card had turned as soft as dough and the writing had dissolved like snow. Good God, what do I do now? I dried the card thoroughly in the sun but then the ink on it turned pale. It looked like a snail had slithered across the card. I traced the words over with fresh ink without changing the writing."

"One day I felt the card and the card was two pieces. After I had held it so much and stuck it into my pocket and pulled it out so many times, a corner of the card had come off and the words 'necessary' and 'bearer' had been erased through finger smudges so that the card was like this: 'Please show all *facilité* to Nafi of this card.' It was meaningless. 'Eh, what can you do?' I said."

"The card was in two pieces. There's this thing called scotch tape; I pasted it back together with that. Now I was so careful with the reference card, you can't imagine. I went back and forth for a month or two but don't think I could ever catch sight of the Director General Bey's face."

"One morning when I was taking the card out of my pocket, I heard a soft ripping noise. I knew what it was, right then. The gum from the tape I had pasted on the card had melted from the heat and had stuck to my picture on my identity papers. When I pulled the card out, the picture was torn out with it. And what part of my picture? It was right in the middle of my face, with the word 'please' stuck on top."

"Now what? I tried to remove the picture but the paper of the card just stuck to it. A friend, to whom I am grateful, said, 'If anybody can do it, so and so can. He is a very skilled master craftsman of phony diplomas,' and he went on to praise the man as well."

"He was supposed to make such excellent phony diplomas

that they surpassed the real diplomas. So I went to the man. 'Since I got out of jail, I've given up doing forgery. I'm into con games now,' he said. 'Oh, please, this isn't forgery. It's a good deed,' I pleaded with him. The man pitied me and started work. While he was working away, suddenly he said, 'What kind of card is this anyway,' and well, sir, there wasn't anything he left unsaid. When he took the picture off, he also removed a layer of paper from the card. The word 'please' went with it. The card said this, 'Show all *facilité* to Nafi Bey of this card'."

"Months went by but I could never get in to see the Director General. The thirteen words on the card had been reduced to nine. If I let more time pass there wouldn't be a single word left on the card."

"Bey Effendi, may Allah persuade you, it was exactly five months...it was in the fifth month. One morning, after I had gone to the government office I pulled the card out of my pocket but what should I see but that the cover of my fountain pen in my pocket had come off and soaked my pocket, and the reference card, in ink. Thank goodness, all of the words weren't covered in ink. Only the word *facilité* was lost."

"One morning I was standing there in the government office all downcast. Someone there said, 'Hey, look! Suppose you get in to see the Director General? What are you going to do?' "

" 'I will say, "I bring the selam of Zeki Bey", that's what I'll say,' I said."

"The man said, 'Whew, somebody brings the selam of Zeki Bey and is kept waiting this long? Seriously, Zeki Bey better not hear about this, how his selam was kept waiting this long, or he'll raise holy hell. If it's Zeki Bey's selam, there's no admission charge. Go on, get on in.' "

"God bless him, that decent fellow got me into the presence of the Director General. I made a bow to the Director General Bey and put my hand into my coat pocket. Alas, my good sir, alas. I don't know why they make men's clothing with so many pockets. A man should have a big pocket like the udder of a maltese goat, tied around his waist, then all he would have to do would be to stick his hand in his pocket to find whatever he wanted. But that isn't the way things are now, sir. First I felt in my pocket. No card. It wasn't in my outer pocket, it wasn't in my handkerchief pocket, it wasn't in the inside or outside pockets of my pants. It wasn't in my pants' back pocket. No reference card. But there was everything else besides the reference card. Streetcar ticket, movie ticket, lawyer's card, toothpick, sesame seeds from a hard roll, oh my goodness! And the more I went on and on fishing through my pockets, the more the Director General laughed. Look here, they weren't like pockets, they were more like the Lost and Found storeroom of the Streetcar Administration Office. Out came buttons, shoe laces, balls of string, anything except my reference card."

"The Director General though it was all a joke. 'Don't get excited. Hunt for it slowly,' he said."

"But before he could finish saying that, what should I see in my hand but the card?"

"The card had stuck to my hand and I hadn't seen it in all my excitement. I handed the Director General the card. He looked and looked at the card but he couldn't read it. He said to one of the officials in the room, 'I can't make that out, read it to me.' The man read out, 'Show all to Nafi Bey of this card.'"

"The Director General said, 'Who is Nafi Bey of this card?'"

"If it was you, what would you say?"

" 'Your humble servant, Effendi,' I said."

" 'Is your family name "Card"?' he said."

" 'It's the family nickname, Effendi,' I said."

" 'I will honor any card from Zeki Bey. Whatsoever there is to show you, I will do it,' he said."

"I was truly sorry that I had found the card. If I had lost it, I wouldn't have had to go through this."

"When I started to say, 'Effendi, Zeki Bey sent your humble servant about a job...' the Director General said, 'I have to tell you that this card is no good for a job but as far as showing you goes, I will show you whatever you want to see.' "

"I left the room, looking over my shoulder. So that was the way it all turned out, Bey Effendi. Now I'm going back to Ankara to get a new card. I will get another card from Zeki Bey because I lost the first one and, please God, I will get a job."

Nafi Bey sighed. I felt sorry for the man. He was going to Ankara for nothing. He would never get the reference card he wanted because that morning I had read in the papers that Zeki Bey had resigned. Nafi Bey must not have read it. I said nothing so that he wouldn't lose his hopes before he got to Ankara.

A Hair From A Toothbrush

("Fırça Kılı", from *Mahallenin Kısmeti,* 1957)

I don't like my uncle at all. He's a stingy fellow. If he hadn't had that terrible illness after he was sixty, we would never have known how rich he was. We had thought that he was middle class like all the other members of our family. When that illness started to torment him and he began to throw away fistfuls of money to save his life, then we saw how rich he actually was. The whole family got angry at the way he had lived like a pauper until he got sick, even though he had money.

My uncle had a pain somewhere between his umbilicus and his lower pelvis but the location wasn't quite clear. Think about the belly and the lower pelvis. There aren't quite forty centimeters between the two of them but in this forty centimeter space the doctors couldn't find where the trouble was for the life of them. The fact that astronomers can tell us the addresses of stars millions of kilometers away off in the heavens but that the doctors couldn't locate where the disease was, between my uncle's belly and pelvis, confirmed my mistrust of medicine.

My uncle would say, "It's as if I had a bunch of dogs and cats in my insides. It's as if you filled a sack with dogs and cats and closed the top and the animals scratched and bit each other. That's the way my insides are scratching."

There is no doubt that there were no dogs or cats inside my uncle. Because he had been a reader of and had written letters to the cultural magazine *Servet-i Fünun* in his youth, he used the literary simile of cats and dogs being in his insides. It would have been better for my uncle if he had had dogs and cats in his insides. Then they could have rescued the poor fellow from his troubles by throwing poisoned pieces of meat to the dogs and cats inside my uncle like the city does to kill ownerless dogs and street cats.

There are a lot of sick people who don't know where their trouble is, so they run to the doctors to learn the addresses of their illnesses, whereas my uncle knew where his disease was.

"Right here," he would say and he would show the forty centimeter place between his belly and his pelvis.

Even though my uncle made things so easy for the doctors, they still could neither find the place of his disorder nor its address.

There wasn't a doctor that my uncle didn't go to. He spent so much money to cure his illness that only then did we see how rich he was.

We had a friend who had been to a professor of medicine who had cured his illness. We immediately took my uncle to this professor of medicine.

As soon as the medical professor had carried out his examination, he said:

"Ulcer!"

We were so happy. It's better for a man to have an ulcer than not to know what is the matter with him.

Relying on the biology I had learned in school, I showed off my knowledge by saying, "My uncle's disease is between his belly and his pelvis. Ulcers are in the stomach. If you were to draw a line from the umbilicus to the sacrum, the stomach would be on top of this line."

However, the doctor said, "You are right but your uncle's

stomach has sagged down. It's three centimeters below that line."

The professor of medicine said that an operation was immediately necessary. My uncle submitted to the operation to escape from the pain and misery. The operation accomplished nothing but increased his misery. I don't know whether this is the truth or not but according to the nurse who was beside the surgeon during the operation, after they sliced open his insides, there was no ulcer in my uncle's stomach.

In fact, the doctor was so surprised that he said, "I've opened thousands of stomachs till today but never in my life have I seen a stomach so healthy."

Seeing this to be the case but so that all his suffering should not be in vain and so that he should at least have earned his fee for the operation, he cut out half of my uncle's stomach and threw it away.

The doctor who was assisting him said, "He hasn't got an ulcer. Why are we cutting up a perfectly healthy stomach?"

But the doctor said, "The stomach is an organ prone to malfunction. Even if he has no ulcer right now, he could have later on. By cutting out and throwing away half of his stomach, we have reduced the danger of his developing an ulcer later by half," thus giving his assistant a new lesson in medicine.

My uncle got up from the operation with a half a stomach but his illness was twice as bad. When this happened, they recommended a specialist to him.

They said, "He's the kind of doctor that, if you haven't been dead for twenty-four hours, he can raise you."

He really was as they had said. As soon as he had examined my uncle, the internist understood in a flash that the disease was in the kidneys.

"You have to have an operation on your kidneys," he said.

They opened my uncle's insides for the second time. With amazement, the doctor saw that the kidneys were perfectly healthy. They were so healthy that he decided that two healthy kidneys were too much for one man, so he took one out and threw it away. It went this way...

One of the young doctors who was performing the operation said, "Why are you cutting out and discarding this absolutely healthy kidney? Good heavens, it works perfectly, like the Greenwich Clock!"

But the internist said, "If we don't take out his kidney, the man will never believe that we've operated on him. They'll say we took his money for nothing. In order not to give rise to any misunderstandings later on, we'll show it to him and say, 'Look, this is the kidney we took out'. We need a piece of evidence," and so saying he cut out one of my uncle's kidneys.

My uncle was so happy to have escaped from the operation with a kidney and that they had not killed him during the operation that, aside from paying them extra money, he put notices in the newspapers expressing his thanks to everybody, from the doctors who performed the operation to the hospital orderlies. Neither the operation nor the letters of thanks helped him. My uncle's pain got all the worse.

An acquaintance said, "I have had sixteen operations. They took out all my organs and put in new ones. It didn't help me in the least. Finally, such and such a doctor cured me."

Immediately, we took my uncle to such and such a doctor. The doctor laughed when my uncle told all the medical adventures he had had.

"They operated on you in the wrong place. You have a knot in your intestines," he said.

I too thought this sounded reasonable. My uncle is so stingy that to avoid extravagance, even his intestines must have knotted themselves up. In fact, they might have gotten themselves into a tangle.

They cut my uncle up for the third time. When he saw his intestines, the doctor was amazed. He tossed the knife and bistoury from his hand and shouted, "What kind of intestines are these? I never in my life saw such long intestines."

My uncle's intestines were long enough to suffice for eight or ten people. I have always resented the inequalities of nature, as far back as I can remember. People's heights, for instance. Some people don't get what they are entitled to and stay short while their leftovers are given to others who just grow and grow. Who knows how my uncle's bowels got this long at the price of how many other people's intestines staying short?

The doctor, although he didn't find the slightest knotting in my uncle's intestines, performed plastic surgery on them with the idea of removing the excess intestines while he had him already there and all opened up.

Even though my uncle's intestines had been reduced to the length of those of a normal person, his illness kept getting much worse.

People recommended a doctor in Ankara to us. They told my uncle, "If he can't cure you, don't try any more. You can't be cured. Just go jump in the sea."

The doctor in Ankara laughed after listening to my uncle's medical adventures. He made his diagnosis in a flash:

"Appendicitis!"

They opened my uncle's belly again and, forget appendicitis and infections, they saw that it was as clean as the heart of an innocent young girl, but because it would have been disrespectful to the art of medicine to have turned back empty-handed, they cut out my uncle's appendix and threw it away.

It was as though this pristine appendix guarded my uncle's health because as soon as they took it out, my uncle's illness got much worse.

After that, my uncle ran wherever and to whomever recommended him a doctor. Every treatment and every operation did nothing but make my uncle's illness worse. I am still amazed at how a civil servant like my uncle could have amassed enough money in his short life to satisfy the doctors. If he had breathed bribes instead of air and eaten them instead of bread, a man could still never accumulate this much money.

There wasn't a place inside my uncle that hadn't been sliced.

All his double organs had been reduced to singles and some had been shortened or any extra part of them had been removed and the ones that did no good like the appendix had been taken out. So, my uncle who had weighed sixty kilos before all these operations, by having his insides emptied out and his double organs reduced to single ones, now was thirty-eight kilos.

Just when my uncle had given up all hope of regaining his health, they recommended him another doctor. They say that where there's life, there's hope. So, my uncle went to this doctor as his last chance.

The doctor laughed bitterly after listening to my uncle's medical adventures.

"What a shame! Your trouble is your tonsils," he said.

"Excuse the question," I said, "but my uncle's trouble is in an unknown point between his kidneys and sacrum. I don't understand how this region is affected by the tonsils."

"I don't understand this very well myself either," the doctor said. "Only basically the tonsils don't serve any purpose. They're superfluous. There is no reason not to take them out. Basically, there is nothing left in your uncle to remove except his tonsils. The malfunction must be the tonsils. Let's take them out and then if he doesn't get better, we can think about it some more."

They took out my uncle's tonsils. This didn't have any effect either. By now my uncle's body had turned into a fish net from all the stitches. The doctors weren't even using knives for the operations any more. They just pulled his stitches open and his insides popped out like a baked eggplant. These stitches served one purpose only: my uncle didn't shout and yell from the pain like he used to because if he strained them just a little bit, they would break open.

By now my uncle was talking nonsense, like "Oh, Lord God, why didn't you create men with zippers from their tops to their bottoms so your servants the doctors could just open them up to have a look?"

One of the doctors who was recommended to my uncle told

him he hadn't a free centimeter of space left in him for an operation.

After saying, "You have a glandular problem. You need hormone treatment. Your hormones are overactive," he said he needed to remove one of my uncle's, if you will excuse me, testicles. To tell the truth, I was surprised that my uncle's hormones could be overactive, with so many of his organs missing, but the doctor said,

"There are no more organs left in his body to work other than the hormone glands so his hormone activity has increased."

Although my uncle pleaded, "Please, take both of them at once so I can be free of all this," the doctor, saying that this would be contrary to medical and humane ethics, only removed one of his testicles.

But this did him no good. Just his testicle was the loser.

Well, sir, just about the time when my uncle was about to kill himself to escape his miseries, a person who had had exactly the same troubles as my uncle and had been cured of them by a certain doctor, gave that doctor's address to my uncle.

The doctor who heard my uncle's medical adventures laughed.

"What a shame," he said. "They could have made another man like you with all the organs they took out of you."

The doctor examined my uncle's feet.

"The trouble is with your feet. I want to cut your calluses off," he said.

To tell the truth, the calluses were the only things my uncle had left to cut off.

In the hope of at least saving his calluses, I shouted, "Doctor, for pity sake, what connection is there between his calluses and the area between his belly and his sacrum?"

"The body is one whole," the doctor said. "If you have an abscess in your little finger, is it only your little finger that hurts or does your whole body from your head to foot feel ill?" he said.

They cut off all of my uncle's calluses. Even if this operation operated to the doctor's advantage, it didn't do anything to help relieve my uncle's illness.

My uncle went over the list of the doctors belonging to the Medical Association. There were only two specialists who hadn't treated him left on the list. First, he went to one. That one was amazed that my uncle was still alive.

"You have ceased to be a human being. Just admire the power of medical science that thanks to medicine you are still alive!" he said.

The last doctor on the list said that the disease was from a dental abcess.

After he had had his teeth pulled in hopes of getting well, he said, "My goodness, I've been emptied out till I feel as though I am going to fly away."

My uncle was alive after a manner of speaking but he had been reduced to a spirit.

One day he said to me, "I want to give my last money to some doctor in Europe."

I went to Paris with my uncle and because we knew no one there, we entered the first place where we saw a doctor's sign hanging over the door. The Parisian doctor listened to my uncle and then examined him. He started laughing. The doctor rolled on the ground laughing. After recovering himself, the doctor took a tweezers.

"Open your mouth," he said to my uncle.

My uncle opened his mouth. The doctor stuck his tweezers in my uncle's mouth, then he pulled the tweezers out.

"How do you feel?" he asked.

My uncle said, "I feel very well. I don't have a pain left."

"Look, this is your problem," the doctor said, showing him a white hair on the point of his tweezers.

"Be careful the next time you brush your teeth. A hair from your toothbrush got stuck in your throat."

We came back from Paris. My uncle had no trace of his illness but he also had no money either. He died, perfectly healthy, six months later. Whether he died from lack of money or because his former operations had left only half of him, I can't say. He couldn't well live on after so many operations, could he?

The Grand Vizier's Donkey

("Sadrazam Eşek" from *Memleketin Birinde,* 1958)

Once upon a time, in the topsy turvy days when grain sieves sat in the straw, there was an Emperor. Like all emperors, this Emperor of a certain country, according to the custom of that era, had gangs of musicians and dancers, harem girls, slave women, servants and yes-men by the score and I don't know what else.

This Emperor in a certain country, like all emperors in all times and in all places, went out hunting when he could spare the time from such important state business as being present at inauguration ceremonies, reviewing parades, reading speeches that other people had written and taking trips.

This hunting fan of an Emperor, because he was very sensitive to humidity, used to call in his Chief Astrologer, before he went on the hunt to kill the special animals which had been specially raised in his special forest, and ask him, "How will the weather be today?" and the Chief Astrologer would always answer his question in the same way, "Your Gracious Majesty, thanks to your kindness, the weather in our country is always bright and sunny. However you command and order, so the weather will be, lord."

The Emperor, who was a suspicious sort like all emperors, did not trust his Chief Astrologer and so he would also ask the Grand Vizier, "How will the weather be today?"

The aged Vizier, the hairs in whose ears had even turned white and with his white beard coming down to his belly, would bow till he touched the Emperor's feet and say, "Thanks to your regal mercies, both at home and abroad, both the political atmosphere and all the other atmospheres, thank God, are very good."

The distrustful Emperor would also ask the other viziers about the weather, one by one, and they would say, "The skyline is pink, the air is clear. May God protect you, could it be otherwise while you reign over us, my lord?"

At last the Emperor would have faith in what all these scientists and statesmen had told him and would believe in his own authority and power and have the hunting gear loaded on the backs of his personal slaves and with the police and gendarmerie going ahead and the sentries coming last and with guards and bodyguards and pickets and rear guards, civilians and state officials and with his cat in the middle of it all and with a great commotion and shouting, laughing and capering, they would set out to hunt his special animals, specially raised in his special forest.

Time came and went and another day the Emperor called in his Chief Astrologer, his Grand Vizier, his viziers, his Chief Molla and his Highness the Foreign Minister, the Chief Eunuch and the Chief Chamberlain and asked them each individually according to their ranks how the weather would be that day and after they had answered, "My lord, thanks to you, the weather today will be better than yesterday," he set out on his way.

Although starting a month beforehand all the roads the Emperor was going to travel over had been combed and any people found on them had been chased off and shooed away, somehow there was still a peasant sitting at the foot of a tree with his donkey.

Because the Emperor had never seen a peasant before in his

life, he could not figure out what sort of creature this ragged, barefooted being might be.

"What are you?" he asked. "Are you a man or a spirit?"

But when the peasant said, "I'm not a man and not a spirit. I'm a person just like you," the Emperor exploded with rage.

"What insolence is this? No one could be like us. Make haste and strike off his head."

But just as the Chief Executioner was bringing down his scimitar towards the hair-thin neck of the peasant, the Emperor shouted, "Stooop! Oh strange being whose talk resembles more or less that of a man, we want to ask you something. If you know the answer we will spare your life. How will the weather be today?"

So the peasant said, "In a little while the wind will blow, a storm will burst, the rain will start and floods will wash everything away."

The Emperor, who was very grieved at these words, shouted, "Traitorous knave, do you not know that when we have willed it, the weather cannot turn bad? How can it rain when the Emperor is hunting? Quick, tie this fellow to the mule's tail."

They tied the peasant's donkey to the tail of a mule and they tied the peasant to the donkey's tail and so they went their way. No sooner had they gone as far as a bullet could fly than the sky suddenly grew dark and was covered with clouds and the lightening flashed and thunder roared and a storm burst forth such that the winds blew from every direction and the floods washed over the earth.

The Emperor who had just saved his life, scarcely managed to stagger into his palace. He was so angry that he fired his Chief Astrologer, his Grand Vizier and his other viziers who had given him the incorrect weather report. Some of them he had beheaded. Then he summoned to his presence the peasant who had warned him that the storm was coming. Giving the Grand Vizier's seal to the peasant who was still shaking and exhausted from having been dragged by the mule's tail, he said, "We make you Grand Vizier."

Some time after he had made the peasant Grand Vizier, the

Emperor had second thoughts and summoned the peasant Grand Vizier into his presence once again and asked him, "How did you know it was going to rain?"

"My lord, when I look at my donkey's ears, I can tell what the weather is going to be like. When it's going to rain, my donkey's ears hang down and I know it will rain that day."

Then the Emperor said to himself, "How stupid of me. So it wasn't the peasant who knew what the weather was going to be, it was the donkey. A donkey knew more than all these viziers and ministers. I have been unjust to this poor donkey. It's not the peasant but the donkey whom I should have made Grand Vizier."

He immediately fired the peasant and made the donkey Grand Vizier. When it was going to be fine weather, the donkey would bray happily, when it was going to rain, his ears hung down and when there would be a storm, his tail hung limp.

When the Emperor was about to proclaim war, set out on a campaign, journey or hunt, he watched the donkey's ears and tail and listened to his braying. He never disobeyed the donkey's bray.

Jesus and Two People

("Hazret-i İsa ile İki Kişi" from
Memleketin Birinde, 1958)

One day Jesus sat in a cafe with a plastic surgeon and a car repairman. Jesus was filling them with religious inspiration. In the course of the conversation the car repairman asked Jesus, "Oh, great teacher, I am consumed with desire to do good to mankind. How can I do good?"

Jesus said, "You must do whatever the Law of the Lord says!"

"By doing good to them that do you evil, you shame them for the evil they have done..." the car repairman said.

The plastic surgeon said, "Man's nature is bad. I speak from experience. Men are bad."

The car repairman said, "No, there is goodness in men. Aren't you the best person in this town of Jericho?"

In fact, the plastic surgeon was the richest man in the city of Jericho as well as the most philanthropic person in town. It amazed the repairman that such a good person would now say that men were bad.

"My case is different," the surgeon said. "I did good to everybody all my life but as recompense I got back evil. This means that men are bad. No one knows this fact better than I do."

Jesus, who had not participated very much in the conversation, drank his wine from his clay jug.

The car repairman said to the plastic surgeon, "If that's so, you'll be all alone in heaven."

The surgeon said, "That's right. That's what I'm afraid of. I'm afraid I'll be bored all by myself up there in that big place."

As a conclusion of this conversation, the repairman made a bet with the surgeon about whether men were good or bad. If the repairman who asserted that men were good won the bet, he would get all the surgeon's property. If he was wrong, the surgeon would take whatever he had.

The three of them came to a place in the country on the road from Jericho to Jerusalem. The plastic surgeon was to stand all alone on this road to see whether the passersby would do him good or evil. Jesus and the car repairman went up to the top of a hill and hid behind an olive tree to watch whatever occurred from a distance.

Both of them prayed to God that what they had predicted would turn out.

The repairman, spreading his hands in prayer, implored, "Oh Lord, if it be Thy will, let them do good unto this surgeon."

If he proved right he would receive the surgeon's private clinic, his mansions, his slaves, his concubines and, most important of all, his five hundred thousand dollar bank account.

"Oh, Lord, if it be Thy will, let people do me evil so that I can get all of the repairman's possessions."

If the surgeon proved right, he would get the repairman's garages, houses, slaves and, most important of all, his hundred thousand dollar bank account.

Footsteps were heard afar off. The surgeon said to himself, "Aha, here comes a robber!"

The repairman said to himself, "Here comes a virtuous person."

A man appeared around the bend in the road. When he had

approached the surgeon, he drew his dagger and shouted, "Out with your money!"

The surgeon was so happy with this that he pulled all of his money out of his pockets, laughing and skipping about.

The robber was amazed at the man's merriment.

"All the years I have been robbing people, I have never seen it make a single one of them happy like it does you," he said.

After that he searched the surgeon from head to foot. Having taken all his money, he was going away when the surgeon called after him, "Mister robber, I have five dollars in my pocket. Would you please take it?"

The robber said, "You must be a religious man. I can see you want to make me ashamed of my deeds but I couldn't care less. Give me that too."

Taking the money, he went on his way. The surgeon called out with joy to the repairman who was hiding behind the olive tree on the hill, "There, you can see with your own eyes that men are bad. You lost your bet and all your property and money are mine."

Jesus spoke to them from the hill in a gentle but deep voice, "Not so fast! Believe that men are good and wait!"

The surgeon started to wait. He heard footsteps again. Both the surgeon and the repairman felt hopeful. One was waiting for a good and the other for a bad man and they implored God that whoever was coming would be what they wanted.

The surgeon said, "Oh Lord, if the man who is coming does me evil, I'll do a good deed by distributing to the poor one fortieth of the property I take from the repairmen."

And the repairman said, "Oh Lord, if the man whose footsteps I hear deals well with the surgeon, I'll give a fortieth part of what I take from him to the poor."

A man came around the bend. When he had reached the surgeon he pulled his dagger and pointed it against his chest and shouted, "Give me your money!"

The surgeon said in joy, "I don't have any money. Search me if you don't believe me but, if you like, you can take whatever else I have of value."

The robber took the surgeon's rings from his fingers, his silver cigarette box, his pen knife and his gold-tipped fountain pen.

When nothing more was left, the surgeon opened his mouth and said to the robber, "Look, look in my mouth, please. I have a gold molar in my upper left jaw. Would it do you any good?"

The robber knocked the surgeon down and pulled out the tooth to get the gold filling. While the surgeon was writhing in agony, he laughed at the same time.

The robber said, "Are you crazy or what?"

He put whatever he took from the surgeon in his pocket and left.

The surgeon shouted to the pair hidden behind the olive tree, "Well, that was somebody who did evil to me. I won. All your property and money are mine."

Jesus called from the hill in a gentle but moving voice, "Be patient. Don't abandon hope and learn to wait."

Another footstep was heard from afar. The surgeon thought, "Here comes another bad person. Who can tell what bad things he will do to me and then I will take all the repairman's money."

And the repairman thought, "It's a good person. Who can tell what kindness he will do to the surgeon? Then I'll take all the surgeon's goods and property and leave him without a penny, hungry and naked."

Someone came around the bend. When he had reached the surgeon, he pulled his dagger and pointed it at his breast, saying, "Gimme the dough! Your money or your life!"

The surgeon said, "Before you came, sir, two respected robbers robbed me. I have nothing left but if you steal whatever I have on, you will make me very happy. My clothes and slippers are new."

The robber took whatever the surgeon had on. He made a bundle of them and was about to go when the surgeon said to him, "Mister Robber, I still have my underpants. Don't you want my underpants? They're very new. This is the first time I've put them on."

The robber said, "You must be a religious fellow but I couldn't care less. Take your underpants off too."

He took his underpants and left the surgeon naked as the day he was born. The surgeon could have flown through the air with joy.

"Hey there," he shouted. "You see, don't you? He did me wrong too. Now all your property and money will be mine."

Jesus said from behind the olive tree in that soft, sweet, but deep voice, "Oh child of God, be patient, wait and do not make haste. Surely a good man will turn up on the face of this earth."

The surgeon started to wait. He heard footsteps. Then a man came around the bend.

The surgeon thought, "The robber didn't leave me with anything that anybody can steal. I hope this is a murderer who wants to take my life. Then I can get all the repairman's property."

The repairman thought, "This must be somebody good. I hope he gives the surgeon a cloth to cover himself with."

From the way the man staggered, it was apparent that he was drunk. He had a club in his hand. When he got to the surgeon, he began to beat him over the head with the club. As the surgeon was being beaten with the club he begged the drunk, "Hit me on the left side. Hit my left shoulder, brother."

When the drunk beat him on the left, he turned his right side to him. The surgeon collapsed to the ground moaning from the pain of the clubbing.

"Mister Thug, please beat me on the head. If it wouldn't be too much trouble for you, please hit my back two or three times more," he said.

"You must be a religious type but I couldn't care less. Here, I'm going to fulfill your desires," the drunk said, and (so saying) he brought his club down again on the surgeon's head.

Then he reeled off.

The surgeon lay where he had fallen, bathed in blood.

He moaned to the repairman, "All your property and money are mine."

Jesus came out from behind the olive tree. He said in that moving, captivating, but deep voice, "Oh child of God, be patient and wait and don't make haste and surely you will find one or two goodhearted people."

They heard footsteps. The surgeon who was groaning on the ground said, "I hope this is a murderer who will want to kill me."

The repairman said, "I hope he helps the surgeon."

A man came around the bend. He knelt by the surgeon who was moaning on the ground.

"What is the matter, brother? Are your wounds very bad?" he said.

The surgeon, seeing that the man wanted to help him and trying to keep Jesus from hearing him, shouted to the man, "Get away!"

The man took wine and olive oil out of his knapsack. He tried to dress the surgeon's wounds. The surgeon, whose nose and mouth were bleeding, shouted, "Get away from me! I don't want your help."

The man said, "How can I not help you if you're suffering?"

He answered, "If you want to help me, clear out of here. In fact, you can plant a kick on my behind as you're leaving, if you really want to help."

"It's our human duty to help one another. Don't keep me from helping you, brother."

The man wanted to dress the surgeon's wounds, no matter what, and carry him to the city on his back.

The surgeon bellowed, "Favors shmeavors, I don't want them! Just get the hell away from me."

When the surgeon saw that he couldn't get rid of the good person, he started to curse the man but he kept right on cleaning the wounds with wine and olive oil and bound them up with his shirt which he had taken off of his back and shredded. The surgeon who realized that he was going to lose all that property and money because of this kindness, painfully got to his feet and picked up a rock from the ground.

Hitting the good man on the head with it, he stretched him on the ground and sat on him.

Jesus and the repairman came down from the hill and went up to them.

The plastic surgeon said to the good man lying under him, "You want to make trouble? Get out of here in a hurry or I'll kill you."

The man, whose head he was beating with the rock said, "I can't go and leave you like this."

The surgeon brought the rock down on his head even harder and left him lifeless. Then he staggered to his feet.

Holding his bloody hands out to Jesus, he said, "I won the bet. Now you see that there are no good men."

The repairman said, "How did you know that?"

The surgeon shouted, "I know it from myself. I know it from myself," and he collapsed to the ground.

The car repairman, in fear of losing all his property and money, threw himself on the wounded surgeon to kill him.

Jesus said, "Take him on your back and carry him to the town and there turn him over to the police!"

One by One, We Fell by the Way

("Hep Döküldük" from *Aferin*, 1959)

I was out of work for a long time, Selim Efendi. Wherever I applied for a job, I came away empty-handed. I was ready to work as a janitor or an office messenger but that wasn't even available. There are six of us, brother. You think it's easy to feed six mouths these days? With the rent money and money just to survive, and the creditors, I was going crazy. And there weren't any savings. Even if there had been, what good would it have done us, Selim Efendi? You can't spend savings forever. We sold off everything we had. There I sat, thinking to myself, "My God, what do I do now?" Not a friend or acquaintance was left from whom we hadn't borrowed money. There wasn't a door left I hadn't knocked on. At last, I started to feel ashamed of myself. On one hand I was angry at my own incompetence. Everybody had found a livelihood and was chugging ahead. I don't think I'm a man who's either incompetent or timid or all that clumsy. I'm as sorry as I can be that I left my old job. Well, I didn't leave of my own free will, they fired me...you know it was nine years I worked in that factory. The owner had to shut the factory down. Raw materials weren't coming from abroad. The man was in the right, of course.

41

He didn't close down all at once. First he let half the workers go. Then he let the administrators go, two by two. Finally, he hung a padlock on the door of the factory.

He called me, "Look here, Izzet Bey," he said, "I'm just about to go bankrupt, today or tomorrow. I'm in the debt of everybody who's worked here but I'm in no shape to pay what I owe. They've even attached my apartment and they're going to sell it very soon. I even sold my car. If you like, I can pay you three hundred liras a month until I go totally broke and you can stay here and work. If you like, I can pay you three months' salary and you can find yourself another job."

When you have a job, you think you can find another any time, any place. And there wasn't anything I didn't say to the fellow. How do you think I could work for three hundred liras, Selim Efendi? The rent alone is three hundred and fifty liras. I raged and ranted and told the boss off. My wages were nine hundred liras. I took my three months pay of two thousand seven hundred liras and walked out.

Before two months had passed, my old boss's business had straightened itself out. He was earning three or four times what he had been making. However, after the way I had talked to him, I was ashamed to ever look him in the face again. There I was, marooned. The money was gone. I was out of work for ten months, Selim Efendi.

I know a young fellow by the name of Burhan. When I say I know him, there is a cafe near our house and I used to go there evenings. I met this Burhan fellow in that cafe. He was a chap I just couldn't stand. He was a brazen, rude dolt who didn't know how to handle himself and talked all kinds of nonsense. Nobody knew just what he did for a living. For a while this Burhan disappeared. Then we heard he was playing party politics. He's a sly dog. He didn't join the government party all at once. He knew that if he joined the government party, nobody would so much as look him in the face. This foxy fellow joined the opposition party first. But if he had only just joined it. . . There wasn't a bad word he left unsaid against the government.Wherever he saw five or ten people together or wherever he saw a square as big as the palm of your hand, there he gave his speech. So the guy got totally out of hand. His pictures and words began to appear in the papers. He was this far from going to prison. Whereas he had it all figured out. Just when he was this far from jail, he sends a telegram to Ankara, saying, "I've seen the light. I've see the path of truth. I kiss your hands in respect." They even read the telegram on the radio. After this, the government party presses him to their bosom like a priceless treasure.

One evening I'm coming home exhausted. I can't tell you how tired I was, Selim Efendi. If somebody had said "Hello" to me, I would have yelled back, "Go to Hell". That day I'd been to seven places to ask for work and in all seven they had gotten rid of me saying, "Leave your address. We'll call you." Whoever I had gone to see to ask for a few piasters loan either hadn't been in or they had said that they didn't have any money. There wasn't even bread at home. I was quivering with nerves. My hands and feet were like ice. Just when I was turning into our street, who should I meet but this Burhan fellow. God knows, I would have tried to pretend not to have seen him but the fellow is nervy. He opened his arms, saying,

"Hey, Uncle Izzet Bey, where have you been? How have you been doing?" and marches up to me, sticking out his hand .

"Very well, thank you," I said, trying to get rid of him.

The brazen, importunate fellow won't let me go.

"I heard you left the factory," he said.

"Yes," I said bruskly and walked on.

"Well, what are you doing now?" he said.

Would I have liked to have punched him in the face?

"What business is it of yours, man? Is what I do any business of yours?"

Never did I see such a persistent, insolent fellow.

"What kind of talk is that Uncle Izzet Bey? Your troubles are my troubles. I really don't have the right to do it but I can be of some small service to you."

I bristled, saying "No thanks, no need."

"Honest, that's no good," he said. "You can't know how much I like you. I heard you were out of work, you were having a hard time. If I were to find you a job at fifteen hundred liras a month, would the money do? Naturally, that would be for the time being. It would be more later on."

I didn't believe him but because a drowning man clings to straws, I said, "Fifteen hundred liras is a lot already."

"Just give me your address."

I gave him my address. Three days later, he came to the house.

"Alright," he said. "I got your business straightened out. You're the chief accountant at X Dam. All you do is write an application letter."

I never thought it would actually happen but I still wrote out the application and sent it in. Fifteen days passed and then the answer came, "You have been appointed chief accountant with the salary of two thousand liras. You are requested to report to work within fifteen days with the accompanying."

It was incredible. If it hadn't been for the official heading of the paper and its date and number, I would not have believed it. He'd said fifteen hundred liras and here were two thousand liras. The whole family danced around the house in joy. Whenever my mother is happy she tells about when she got married and then there's a folk song, "Jingle jangle, down the stairs", she starts to sing that. When she heard that I had got a two thousand lira job, she started to tell about when she had been a bride.

"Oh, mother, forget all about this bride business and make us some tea," I said.

"Alright, son," she said and snapping her fingers and singing the "Jingle jangle, down the stairs" song, she went into the kitchen.

The next day we began to smarten up a little. True, I had found a two thousand lira a month job but how were we six people to get there? If we went with our odds and ends, it would cost at least a thousand liras travel fare. We didn't have even ten liras. If I went on alone and sent for the family later, they wouldn't have enough money to survive even for one day here.

In the ten months I had been out of work, there wasn't anybody I hadn't asked for a loan. I'd asked for money from everybody. I stuffed the paper from the dam in my pocket and hit the streets to ask for a loan. Selim Efendi, not a thousand liras could I not find. I couldn't get my hands on a hundred liras. Fifteen days went by, twenty days went by. An official letter came from the dam.

"This is to inform you that as you have not yet started your job, that if you do not start work within the next ten days, someone else will be appointed to your post."

I was a hair's breath from going crazy. I had found a two thousand lira job but, just imagine, I couldn't go and take it. I begged and pleaded but to no avail. Nobody would give me ten piasters. Two more weeks went by. Then another paper came, "This is to inform you that if you have not taken up your post in one week, the appointment will be invalidated."

The place we had to go was five days journey from here. I saw there was no hope from anybody. There wasn't a thing in the house left to sell off. I said, "Let's sell the bedding and quilts and clothes." The very next day we sold everything we had and were left with just what we stood up in. We had four hundred liras in our pockets. I went immediately to get the tickets and we spent that night in a hotel. The train was supposed to leave at five o'clock the next afternoon. When it was still morning, my mother began to cry, "Hurry up, let's go."

"Where are we going, dear? It's nine hours till the train leaves"

"I don't care. You don't know Istanbul like I do. People can't go from one neighbor to another in nine hours."

It was nine o'clock. Now my wife started in.

"Hurry up. Let's go."

"You want to wait in the station for eight hours in this cold?"

"Anything could happen. There could be some sort of accident!"

If we didn't catch this train, I'd lose the job. Anyway, we'd have gone all the way there for nothing. If we caught this train, I'd just show up barely in time to claim the job. My son and daughter now started to mutter,

"Come on, daddy, let's go. Come on, daddy, let's go."

Despite everything, I too began to feel anxious. We left the Sirkeci hotel at 10 o'clock in the morning. We would go to Haydarpaşa Station to catch a train that was leaving seven hours later.

We hadn't walked a hundred feet before some fellow started following my daughter. The guy made fresh remarks to her without stopping:

"Eat me up, honey..."

I kept on saying to myself, "Lord, give me patience". My son started to clench his fists.

My mother was saying, "Son, don't play into the ruffian's hands. If we miss the train, we're ruined."

The fellow wouldn't leave my daughter alone.

"Sweety, let me lie down and you mash me."

This was what you call trouble with bells on.

"Oh, mama. Please, pretty please."

My daughter had turned ashen grey.

On the one hand I was trying to calm down my son, saying, "Watch out, son. Don't play his game" and on the other side, I was trying to pacify my daughter, saying, "Just don't pay any attention, daughter."

But it wasn't enough for him to rag her. The fellow had to lay his hands on my daughter, right in front of everybody. It must have hurt my daughter because she gave a scream as if her flesh were being ripped away. A crowd and surrounded us and the police came too. Damn it all, just think. They were going to take the molester and my girl to the police station. The poor girl was crying.

"Daddy, don't let me keep you from your trip. You go on and hurry to your train. If I can, I'll come to the station after you. If I can't, I'll take the train tomorrow. You go on now."

My heart was torn to pieces but what can you do, Selim Efendi? I gave my daughter one hundred and fifty liras and said,

"Whatever you do, daughter, follow us."

After the girl left us, we were five people. We went on our way. Before we had gone a hundred steps, who should cross our path but a drunk. The fellow couldn't stand up. His eyes were glazed. He was slobbering.

He opened his arms wide, saying, "Oh, Mommy, I though you were dead. You left me an orphan all these years. Where did you come from now?" He fell all over my wife.

"Mister, get away from here. We're busy."

The drunk wasn't the kind you could talk to. I could barely restrain my son.

"How could you have left me six months old in my swaddling clothes and run off with another husband?" he said, throwing himself on my wife.

This is how trouble just finds a man out, Selim Efendi, no matter what. A crowd gathered around us. There was no way to save my wife from the drunk. He was feeling her all over and kissing her, "smack, smack, smack".

He never stopped saying, "How could you leave me an orphan all these years?"

"Mister, get away from us, for pity sake. My wife's thirty five. How could she be your mother?"

The drunk wound himself around my wife. The poor woman struggled with all her might. They ended up rolling on the ground. Thank goodness, the police came and arrested the drunk. Then off to the police station. The poor woman's eyes streamed tears.

"Don't let this keep you from going," she said. "Go on, for pity sake. If I can, I'll catch the train. If not, I'll take the train tomorrow."

What else could I do, Selim Efendi? I had been out of work

for eleven months. Could I lose out on a two thousand lira a month job? I gave my wife two hundred liras. Off they went to the police station. On we went having lost two casualties from our family. Thank goodness it wasn't worse. Before we had gone a hundred steps, a fellow steps in front of my son, shouting "Hey, you!"

"For mercy's sake, son, don't give in to him!"

All the same, the fellow was a bully. He wouldn't leave my son alone. He kept on after him.

"Mister, go on about your business. We don't know who your are and we don't want to."

He grabbed my son by the collar and asked him, shaking him all the time, "Aren't you a man, damn it?"

"I'm a man, so what?"

"I ... men like you..."

If you had seen the bully, he was a scarecrow. My son, may Allah protect him, if he had given a hard cough, he would have finished the bully off.

"Mister, please, you don't know what's going on. It's a life or death situation. We've got to catch a train. Let us alone."

He wouldn't let go.

Saying, "Men like you, I ..." he spits a wad of phlegm!

My son was about to cry.

"Daddy, don't you miss the train. Hurry up, you go on. I'll catch up with you if I can. If I can't, I'll come on with the train tomorrow. Now I *have* to beat the stuffing out of this guy."

I gave the boy a hundred liras. The boy put the hundred liras in his pocket and, calling on Allah's name, he lit into the bully. He started to knead him like dough. In the meanwhile the police came up. We left the boy and went on.

We had lost three people from our family. On our way we went.

My mother said, "We've had a fifty per cent casualty rate."

I looked at my watch. It was one-thirty. Before I could say, there's three and a half hours till the train, Selim Efendi, what should come towards us but a truck big as a monster. First it hit the electric light post. It went right over the light post. It didn't slow down and tossed a car thirty feet away. Away we run and here the truck comes, right after us. It crushed five or six people. First we climbed up on the sidewalk. Then we ran into a barber shop. But the truck came and poked itself into the barber shop as if it had a blood feud with us. I heard a scream. The truck had run over my little girl.

Just think about it, Selim Efendi. We weren't fated to get from Sirkeci to Haydarpaşa in one piece.

The police came. They made some phone calls. Anyway then, the ambulances came. The injured were put in the ambulances.

Because she knew what I had suffered from being out of work, my poor child said from the stretcher she was lying on, "Daddy, don't let this keep you from going. I'll come along later."

My mother started to cry. Even if we were left, we would be completely miserable. I gave my daughter a hundred liras. The ambulance went off. All that was now left was me and my mother, two people. My family had all fallen by the wayside. My mother and I were dashing along.

At a certain point while my mother was saying, "For gracious sake, son, keep a tight hold on yourself. Let's get to that dam before something happens to us," suddenly the sound of her voice was cut off. I looked and my mother was gone.

I started shouting, "Moother, moother," in the middle of the street.

Had this woman flown away? She had been right there beside me. I shouted, "Moootheer" with all my voice.

The woman had disappeared. Everyone gathered around me. Someone in the crowd said, "Be quiet. I hear a voice."

We all strained our ears. A voice was coming from far away and from the depths as though it were coming out of the bottom of a well, "Izzet, Izzet."

What should we see when we looked where the voice was coming from but that my poor mother had fallen into a hole that the road repairmen had dug?

We stuck a ladder down but it wasn't long enough. We let a rope down but my mother couldn't climb up it. My poor old mother had sunk into the mud in the hole. "We can't save this woman with the aid of the Municipality. We have to call for help from the Department of Housing," they said. My poor mother called up from the bottom of the hole,

"Son, you go on. Go on, don't you be late. For heaven's sake, don't miss your train or you'll lose your job. Go on, hurry. If it's my fate to get out of here, I'll follow you."

I threw my mother a hundred liras. I started scurrying. It was three-thirty. There was an hour and a half till the train left. I was praying, "Allah, don't let me have an accident on my way."

Out of a six person family that had fallen by the way, only I was left. I got on the boat. Thank goodness, I got over to Haydarpaşa. I decided to buy some little cakes to have something to eat on the way, on the train. A young guy ahead of me bought a cookie from the cake salesman. When he picked it up, he bit into the cookie. He gave the salesman twenty-five piasters. The salesman said,

"Fifty piasters."

The young fellow got mad.

"What'd you mean, fifty piasters. These cookies cost fifteen piasters. You gotta give me back ten piasters."

They started to fight. In the meantime, a crowd had gathered. Then what should the young guy say to the salesman but, "I gave you a lira"?

They lit into one another.

The youth asked the salesman, "What the hell is your name anyway?"

And the salesman said, "Evangeli."

No sooner had he said this, than the youth turned to the crowd and began to shout,

"You, fellow citizens, you're all witnesses. This man has insulted the Turkish race. I am a Turkish youth. By calling me a liar, he has insulted the Turkish race."

As soon as they heard this, the crowd dispersed. Everybody ran in a different direction.

The youth hollered, "Police, police!"

He said to the police that came, "This man's insulted the Turkish race."

Then, pointing to me, he said, "And this gentleman's a witness."

The police grabbed me by the hand. God Almighty...I begged the policemen, "For God's sake, Mr. Policeman, I have to catch a train. I'm in a hurry. Let me go. It's a life or death business."

"You're going to the police station."

"I didn't even hear a thing."

"You can tell that at the station."

Oh, God above! There was a half an hour till the train left. We went to the police station. I was about to cry. I begged the police captain, "I'm begging you, let me go. If I don't catch this train, my whole family will suffer. My life will be ruined."

The police captain was a kindhearted man.

"I understand you, my friend, but I can't help you. If this were a private matter, I would let you go but you are a witness to an offense against the state."

I was all but crazy, Selim Efendi.

"So, what's going to happen?"

"First, I'll check your ID. Then I'll take your testimony. After that, you'll give your testimony in a summary hearing."

Look, Selim Efendi, did you ever hear of such a mess? My whole future was ruined. There was nothing to do but to escape. When the captain turned his head, I came to life. I started running like you never saw. As soon as I started running, whistles began to blow. I'm running this way and that in that big old station. In an instant the station was full of police. They were all running after me. I ducked two policemen who ran out in front of me and took off for the train. That stinking train wouldn't leave. If it would leave, I'd be safe. I dived in one end of the train. The police were coming right after me. I'm running like anything and the police are blowing their whistles, "tweet, tweet."

They're running after me, shouting, "Get him, get him."

There's ten minutes left till the train leaves. On and on I run. Then I turn around and run back into the station. I don't know which way to turn to keep from getting caught. I dived into the station's public toilets. I went into an empty booth and immediately bolted the door behind me. Right afterward the police started to run up and down the corridor between the toilets.

Yelling, "Where is he? Where did he go?" they started beating on all the toilet doors.

Every time they beat on the door, voices would come from inside,

"Cough-cough."

"It's full."

"There's somebody inside."

They beat on my door.

I called out, "Occupied."

I heard the police talking outside.

One of them said, "Three of you wait out here. He came in, so he's got to come out. Then you'll catch him."

I was going off my rocker, Selim Efendi. There were three minutes till the train left, two minutes, one minute. I opened the door and shot out as fast as I could. The police grabbed onto me, one of them by my pants leg, one of them by the tail of my coat, one of them by my collar. Out of there we came. And the train went "tooot"...and left.

When the train left, I relaxed. They took me to the station. The captain said with a frown,

"You are a witness to an offense against the state, sir. You're not a suspect. So why then did you run off?"

What had happened, had happened.

"It's not that I ran off. It's that I had to go to the bathroom."

The captain said,

"Bring in the suspect."

The police went out. After a while they came back and said,

"He's gone, sir."

"What do you mean, 'He's gone'? If he's gone, then bring in the plaintiff."

The police went out and then came back in.

"He's gone, sir. Both of them have run away."

The captain got mad. He turned on me.

"It's all your fault. Why did you run away? We let the suspect and the plaintiff both get away while we were trying to catch you. You go on and get out too now," he said.

So it happened, Selim Efendi. I missed the train and lost my job. My little daughter and my mother were in the hospital. My wife and the other daughter are staying in the house of a friend. My son is in prison. I'm on my way to visit him there now. So good-by now, Selim Efendi.

Bravoo

("Aferiiin" from *Aferin*, 1959)

Where was there a friend to hand me that much money for a loan on a tray? I had started collecting two and three hundred lira loans at a time from my friends. I was filling up my briefcase with the money I had collected. The book had been typeset in the printing house and then printed and was waiting for me. The press owner was rushing around looking for me to get his money. And I was running right and left to raise the money through loans.

The printer was looking for me and I was looking for the money and so one evening I came home with around three thousand liras in my briefcase. The money which I had collected from here and there, little by little and bit by bit was in two and a half lira pieces, five lira pieces, ten lira pieces and the biggest size was a fifty lira bill. Because of this, the three thousand-odd liras, like any little thing that wants to look big, was swelling and puffing itself up. I could hardly stuff the money into my briefcase.

In the morning I stuffed this brazen money into my briefcase and set out early for the press. I was going to take it straight to the printer and pick up my books.

My briefcase has become something like my hand, like an organ, from carrying it around all these years. I can't keep my balance without my briefcase in my hand. If I don't have my briefcase, I lose my balance and walk along leaning over to one side.

I came to the pier. The ticket window was closed. I waited in the waiting room. I put the bag behind me, inside the window. I leaned the back of my neck on the briefcase so I wouldn't forget it. I was reading the newspaper. The waiting room was full. The doors opened. I went, got my ticket and got on the boat. Well, there were a lot of people who knew me. I greeted people right and left. The greeting of a man with three thousand liras in his briefcase is a different sort of greeting.

"Hello."

"How do you do, sir?"

"Good morning, sir."

"Good morning."

Since I've said this much, I may as well tell everything. I was looking for a good looking woman to sit across from. I swear it wasn't with a bad intention. It was to make the woman happy and to please my eyes as well...But the woman who sat across from me must have been displeased by the sight of me. I wasn't thinking much about that end of it.

Anyway, the sharp operators had grabbed all the seats in the boat across from the good looking women. I had no luck at all. All that was left was an empty seat across from an ugly woman. It was as if they'd reserved me a numbered seat just to make me unhappy. Why, my friend, the woman was so ugly that you couldn't even do her the courtesy of looking her in the face to please her. The woman was so gosh awful ugly that even when I held my paper over my face, I still could see her. She wasn't a woman. She was a blessed "undying memory". Once you had looked at her face, you'd never forget it as long as you lived. God knows, she probably thought the same about me. While I was plotting how to get out of this difficult situation, who should I see but Her on a bench on my right side?

As soon as I saw Her, my heart hopped into my mouth.

Exactly twenty-three years, I hadn't seen her. Allah be praised, here She was! It was obvious from everything about Her that She was the wife of an important man. You know, it's like they say of healthy, lively people, "The color was just dripping from her face." It wasn't just the color from Her face but oil and honey.

First of all, I better tell you who She was. Once, She was a fresh young girl. I wasn't Her beloved but She was mine. I was crazy for this girl. This girl never once out of kindness so much as looked at me. Later on, I had my people ask her mother for the girl's hand in marriage. Her mother, the brazen female, shamed us in front of the whole neighborhood by turning the proposal down, saying, "I won't give my daughter to a man with no future."

And that "She" was the "She" right here. I saw that four people were sitting on a bench big enough for five. I immediately got up across from the ugly woman, saying "Excuse me, please," to a fat man who was sitting there, and then squeezed in at Her side.

"How do you do, ma'am?" I said.

I don't care what she may have been but She was a polite woman.

"Thank you. How are you, Sir?" She said.

"*Merci.* Do you know who I am?"

"Why of course. How could I not know you?"

Once upon a time when She was a girl, She wouldn't pay any attention to me and her mother hurt my feelings. Now my intention was to get my revenge. Eh, I was pretty well known. Everybody knew me. Who knows, the woman was probably thinking to herself, "Why did I make such a mistake and not marry this fellow?" That is, I was thinking that she was thinking this. While I was thinking thus, what should She ask but, "What work do you do?"

Umph, my God, if a writer's old sweetheart doesn't know what kind of work he does for a living, you can pretty much keep that kind of fame. I was very put out.

Puffing myself up a little bit, I said, "I am a writer."

Opening her mouth wide, she said, "Is that so? You mean you never found a proper job? What a shame."

The woman was making fun of me.

"Are you married?" I said.

"I'm married. And yourself?"

To irritate the woman, I looked to one side and said, "I'm married. Do you have any children?"

"I do."

If she had said, "No", I would have said, "Oh, really? I have children."

"How many children do you have?"

"Five."

The woman had one up on me again. I have four children.

She opened her eyes wide.

"You should say, 'May Allah keep them from harm.'"

"May Allah keep them safe."

"Who is your husband?"

She said the name of her husband. Her husband was somebody whose name people would immediately recognize. If twenty-six million people don't know it, then at least twenty million do.

Stubbornly, I asked, "What does he do? What line's he in?"

She ignored my question, as if to say, "You don't show any respect for my husband, so..."

"He's in Europe right now."

Pouting my mouth and striking a romantic pose, I said, "Are you happy at least?"

If she had said, "I'm not happy," I would have done a little belly dance right there in my seat.

"And how!" she said.

"What do you expect? Unfeeling woman, that's all anybody would expect from you. You don't have any feelings, of course you're happy," I said to myself.

She asked me, "Are *you* happy?"

"O-o-oh, I'm so happy you can't imagine."

"Have you had an accident?"

"You're too kind..."

You don't say, "You're too kind," when somebody asks you if you've had an accident but I was confused. I said that out of my bewilderment.

"I looked at you a little while ago and you were walking all lopsided."

As soon as the woman said this I groped around with my hand and then I shouted, "Oh no, I'm ruined!"

I don't walk lopsided. It must mean that I was missing my briefcase and I had been walking leaning over to one side.

I kept shouting, "I'm ruined, I've had it. Help!" She, however, kept on laughing at me. Everybody was laughing at me for the way I had hopped up while the woman was sweetly talking to me about whether "I was happy" and so on.

I ran to the ugly woman across from whom I had got up.

"Madam, did I leave a briefcase here?"

The ugly woman couldn't answer me for laughing. I ran from one side to the other. And all the time I was shouting, "Help, I'm ruined!"

"What is the matter, sir? What's your problem?"

"I've lost my money."

I don't know if this has ever happened to you but at times like this, you don't think about your own stupidity or forgetfulness. You only think about other people's wickedness.

"My money has been stolen," I shouted.

She, doubled up with laughter, asked me, "Was it a lot, at least?"

"Three thousand liras."

"I thought it was a big amount. My goodness, is it worth having a stroke over three thousand liras?"

"There were three thousand liras but there were ten thousand liras besides."

There is no mercy left in the hearts of men. My three thousand liras had disappeared, I was in misery and they were laughing at me. If they had had a shred of mercy, they would have pitied me and taken up a collection of three thousand liras for me.

On top of that, while I was trying to show off in front of Her, I had made a complete fool of myself.

Somebody asked me, "Who do you suspect?"

"Who do you think? I suspect everybody, including the captain," I shouted.

One of the passengers said, "Did they take it out of your pocket?"

"No, it was in my briefcase."

"Are you sure you haven't left it outside?"

All of a sudden I pulled my wits together and leapt up. The bag was in the waiting room.

The boat was about to sail. They had untied the cables. It was leaving the dock. The boat was starting to move out to sea.

"Watch out, you'll fall."

"Stop, for God's sake."

"Don't jump! What are you doing?"

But who's to listen? I gave a running jump and flung myself forward. I didn't jump, my two hands became two wings and I flew. I must have broken a long jump record but nobody knows about it.

As soon as I got onto the dock I started to yell, "Bag, baaag!"

I looked into the window where I had left my bag but it wasn't there.

"The bag. You know, the bag. Hasn't anybody seen it?"

A newsboy said, "What kind of bag was it, uncle?"

"What do you mean what kind? It was just a plain, ordinary bag."

"Was it new?"

"Eh, it was fairly new."

"What color was it?"

"Coffee color."

"Was it big?

"Medium size."

"I swear, I ain't seen it, uncle."

"God damn your hide. Bag, bag!"

A voice rose from the crowd.

"I saw it. The dock hand took it."

Now I started yelling, "Dock hand, dock haand!"

Once more someone from the crowd said, "He gave it to the dockside bo'sun."

I relaxed a little.

"Where is the bo'sun?"

"Is it the bag? Was it yours?"

"Yes, the bag. It's mine."

"The bo'sun gave it to the supervisor."

"The supervisor?"

"The supervisor took the bag to the police station."

The police station was on the square by the quay. I shot out like an arrow. My heart was like a bird, ready to flutter out of my mouth.

I ran up the stairs two and three at a time and flung open the first door.

"Bag!" I cried.

A doctor who was vaccinating a child said, "What bag?"

"My bag."

"What happened?"

"I lost it."

"When?"

"Will you please stop all the questions, mister? Where is the bag?"

"Look upstairs. This is the city clinic."

After opening a couple of doors, I found the police station. There were four policemen in the first room I went into. I shouted, "Baag!"

"What bag?"

"The superintendent found it and he brought it here."

"Look in the police superintendent's office. In the next room."

I flung the door of the next room open so fast that the people inside should have stuck their hands in the air in surrender.

Both the money and the briefcase were on the table. The two and a half pieces, the pieces of five, the ten bills had all swollen up and made a hill. It looked as though it were three hundred and not three thousand liras. The bag was on the table. The police superintendent, the police captain, the dock official and the bo'sun were all there, counting the money.

"That money is mine. The bag is mine, too. I forgot it on the dock."

The superintendent said, "How do we know that the bag is yours?"

"I will prove to you that the bag is mine in a way that nobody else could prove that the bag was his. There is a piece of paper with writing on it in the bag. Take the piece of paper out."

The superintendent took out a piece of paper that I had put in the bag to give to a newspaper that day.

"Yes."

"I will now tell you from memory what is written on that piece of paper."

The police superintendent took the piece of paper in his hand, "Tell me," he said.

"The title of the article is 'The Government is on the Wrong Path.'"

"Yes," the police superintendent said.

The captain didn't believe it. He bent down and read the article the superintendent was holding.

" 'The Government is on the Wrong Path.' "

"Isn't that right?" I said.

"That's right, 'The Government is on the Wrong Path.' "

"Isn't that enough. What more do you want?"

"Somebody else could say that. Everybody says it. Read the rest."

I recited the article as best I remembered it, " 'In the time of the old regime, citizens were beaten in the police stations. Having achieved a democratic regime, we hoped that the beatings in the police stations would be abolished. However, under the new administration, citizens are being beaten in the police stations.' Is that right, sir?"

The superintendent of police who had been reading the piece of paper while I was talking, said, "That's right, sir, it's correct."

"Did I make a mistake?"

"You did, but it's not important. You said, 'Citizens are being beaten in the police stations.' "

"That's right, isn't it?"

"It's right but," (reading the article), " 'in the police stations citizens are being beaten'. First 'police stations', then comes 'citizens'."

"I should think that you know that the bag is mine by now."

"Not really. Go on. Anybody could say that."

At a certain point when I was reciting my article from memory, the police superintendent said, "Yes, alright."

About the middle of the article, the police superintendent frowned.

I asked once more, "Isn't that right?"

The police superintendent roared, "What do you mean? Of course it's not right."

"I mean, isn't that what's written in the article in your hand?"

"What if it's written in the article? Does that make it true?"

Things were getting sticky. Here I had come of my own free will to the police station to get back my three thousand liras and now suppose then and there they were to write a report that I had libeled the government and send me to court?

I had come to the end of the article. Everybody was scowling.

"Now you know that it's my bag," I said.

The police captain said, "We know."

He turned to a policeman.

"Make out a form and give him his bag."

We went into the next room. A clerk started to write out a form on the typewriter. Dock official and the bo'sun hovered

around me, waiting. Why didn't they go about their busi-
nesses? They had found the bag. They had taken it to the
police station. All right, what more did they want?

I knew what they wanted but it made me nervous to have
them hovering around me. The clerk was writing the form.
They were hovering around me and I was thinking,

"How much money should I give them? The one who found
the money was the bo'sun. I'll give him a hundred liras. The
official didn't do a thing. He didn't do anything but I'll give
him fifty liras anyway. No, fifty isn't enough. An official is an
official. He's superior to the bo'sun. I have to give him a
hundred liras. But I can't give away a hundred piasters of this
money. It's not my money, it's a loan. But if it is a loan, so
what? What if they had kept the money themselves. I'll lose
two hundred liras for no reason. It will be the penalty of my
stupidity. OK, but these men are hovering over me. what do
they want? I'll give them two hundred liras each. It's not much
but I'll put a 'thank you' notice in the papers. And in addition
I'll write a letter to their boss at the Maritime Bank and tell
about their good deed. One hundred liras is too little. If they
print in the paper that 'a man who lost three thousand liras
gave the bo'sun who found it one hundred liras,' people will
say, 'Ptuh! Brazen, stingy guy.' Nobody would know that the
money was loans from all over. The best thing to do is give
them two hundred liras apiece. No, no, two hundred and fifty
liras."

While I was thinking all this, the receipt had been written
out. The policeman wanted my ID.

"I don't have my ID on me."

"Well, bring it. We can't give it to you if you don't have your
ID."

"Why?"

"What if somebody comes and says the money is his?"

"Couldn't he still say that even if I had my ID?"

"Yes, but we need to know who we gave that money to. If you
don't have your ID, how do we know who you are?"

"I'm in a hurry. That bag couldn't belong to anybody else. Could anybody else repeat the article you took out of the bag?"

"You're right. We believe you but..."

The hours were passing. The bo'sun was long gone but the official hung around me. There was no way he would go away.

They asked the police superintendent.

"Give it to him," he said. "Nobody else's going to claim the bag."

The police were about to give it to me but now the dockside official said, "You can't do that, sir."

"Mister, what business is that of yours? You found a bag. You took it to the police station. Your business is finished."

"Not in the least!"

"Isn't that the truth, my friend? Why are you interfering with whether they give me the bag or not?"

"No, sir. I can't be responsible."

"How on earth is it your business, brother?"

The police on the one hand and I on the other plead with the dock official.

The police said, "What shall we do?"

The official said, "Just let me phone Operations."

Aha, now I understood. The official was going to tell his bosses he had found a bag with three thousand liras and taken it to the police station to let them know what a good boy he was so that they would write "bravooo" in his record. That was what he wanted. That was why he acted so contrary.

Whereas, if he hadn't been so difficult, I would have printed a letter of thanks in the newspapers, I would have expressed my thanks to his bosses and I would have shamefacedly begged him to be so kind as to accept two hundred and fifty liras from me.

"Please, sir, I'm in a hurry."

"No sir. I have to phone my superiors."

I laughed, "Very well. I'll bring my ID and get the money tomorrow. You go phone your bosses so they can tell you 'Good boy!'"

I left. The next day I got my bag from the police station.

Now whenever the dock official sees me, he whispers something to the people beside him.

The other day, a friend of my mine on the boat said, "What you did was a shame."

"What did I do?" I asked.

"Why you lost your bag. It had three thousand liras in it and you didn't even give them thirty liras."

"Sure I didn't," I said. "You would have to give at least six hundred thousand liras to the honest man who returned three thousand liras to the owner. I don't have that kind of money!"

Does Anybody Know Pumpkin Muammer?

("Kabakçı Muammer'i bilen var mi?" from *Aferin*, 1959)

Somebody was saying over the phone, "I've been looking for you all week."

He had already told me his name. It was Muammer. He was talking to me over the phone as though I knew him.

"Excuse me, sir. Who are you?" I asked him.

And he said once more, "Muammer."

It would have been rude to have asked "What Muammer?" What if he were somebody that I should definitely have remembered, that is, if he thought I should have?

"I asked everybody. Finally somebody gave me your telephone number."

Hesitantly, I said, "What can I do for you, sir?"

"I have to talk to you."

"Go ahead, sir."

"Not on the phone. Where's your house?"

Finally, I said, "Excuse me but I don't know who you are."

"You don't know me? That's a shame...Don't you know my voice?"

"No, I don't recognize it?"

"I'm Muammer, darn it all."

"What Muammer, sir?"

"Muammer number 195. Weren't we classmates? Pumpkin Muammer."

"Ohh, is that you then, Muammer?" I said but I still didn't know who he was. It would be very rude not to pretend that I knew him. He must have been a friend from high school.

"Well, it's me," he said.

Twenty-six years had passed since I had finished high school. How could I remember Pumpkin Muammer?

"Look, something very important is going on. I have to see you right away. Give me your address."

I gave him directions to my house. He came in the afternoon. As soon as he got inside the door, he hugged me around the neck. Well, after all weren't we school buddies? I wanted to put my arms about his neck but I couldn't very well do it. He stood over six feet high. All I could do was put my arms around his waist. He kissed me on either cheek in greeting, "smack," "smack." I hopped up and down a couple of times but because I couldn't reach his cheeks, I pursed my lips and made a "mump", "mump" noise in the air twice and that's how I kissed him.

I turned around and wiped my cheeks off. I never saw a fellow kiss like that. My cheeks were sticky as if they had been licked by a water buffalo. He went over to the armchair and sat down. We sat there and looked at one another. I couldn't remember any such a friend. I thought and thought but I couldn't think who he might be. For one thing, there was nobody so tall at our school.

There we sat, looking at one another. We looked and looked at each other.

"You probably don't know me," he said.

If I said I didn't know him, it would have been very rude. You don't forget your school chums.

"I know you, man. You think I wouldn't know you?"

"So who am I?"

"Muammer."

"What Muammer?"

"Pumpkin Muammer."

"Uh-huh, now I believe you. If you had said, 'I don't know you,' I'd have spat 'Ptuh' right in your face and walked out."

"I know you, I know you. You're Pumpkin Muammer."

"Now listen to me, buddy. I'm in trouble and only you can save me. You know a lot of people. I'm really in trouble, my friend."

"Tell me all about it Muammer. Go on and tell me."

"You know I went to America to study chemical engineering."

I knew no such a thing but I said, "I know, Muammer, buddy."

"I don't know whether you heard or not but you must have heard that I fell in love with a girl in America."

"I heard, Muammer."

"The girls' father was a hotel manager. I married this girl. You must know about it."

"I know, Muammer."

"Then, my friend..."

He kept on talking away and I kept on peering at his face trying to figure out who he might be. Every so often he would stop his chatter and say, "Damn it all, you don't know who I am!"

"I know you, buddy. I know you. I swear it."

"So if you know me, why do you keep looking at me like an ox?"

"I'm, that is, I'm listening to you."

"Have you gotten too good for me?"

"God almighty, why would I have gotten too good for you, Muammer. Go on, I'm listening."

"Well, then I married this girl and two months after I got married, I got sick. You must have heard about it."

"I did, Muammer."

"You're telling a lie."

"Why should I lie? I did hear, I swear."

"If you heard, tell me. What was the matter with me?"

"What did they say the other day? Ulcers, appendicitis? What did they say it was?"

"Wrong."

"I don't rightly remember. What *was* it then, Muammer?"

"How do I know? Nobody had a clue. None of the doctors could diagnosis it. Then they said you have to have an operation. I had the operation. You must have heard."

"Now that I didn't hear."

"Damn it, are you my friend or not? If I die in a foreign country, you wouldn't even know about it."

"Buddy, I have to tell the truth about this. I heard whatever I heard and I didn't hear what I didn't hear."

"So you didn't hear? Well anyway...I had a brain operation."

"I'm glad that that's over with."

"After the operation I couldn't go back to university. So my father-in-law said, 'You best go to hotel management school here. I'll give you the money,' he said. 'Then you can take your wife and go back to Turkey and open a hotel there,' he said. I said OK. Then I started to take a correspondence course in hotel management. I corresponded for two years with this hotel school. They sent me my diploma after two years. I graduated first in the class from this hotel school. I got my diploma. My father-in-law said, 'Get some training and really learn the hotel business.' 'How?' I said. I was supposed to start in the maintenance in the hotel my father-in-law managed and then go on and work as a waiter. 'Shall I study waiting on tables by correspondence?' I asked him. 'You can't do it my correspondence,' he said.

All the while he was talking away, I was looking at him, trying to figure out who he was.

All of a sudden, he interrupted himself and shouted, "Damn it, you still don't know me."

"I know you, I swear to God, Muammer."

"So, if you know who I am, why are you looking at me like an ox in the field?"

"It's because I'm listening carefully."

"You don't know me but never mind...Then after that, I started to do the cleaning in the hotel. There were twenty cleaning people in the hotel. I was originally supposed to have done cleaning for four months. Before a week was up, the cleaners started saying, 'For heaven's sake, get this guy out of here.' I understood what it was. The guys were jealous of me. They couldn't say anything right out because I was the manager's son-in-law. They started complaining, 'He knows the cleaning business better than we do. Please, get him out of here.' So I was promoted one level. They put me at the hotel switchboard. Fourteen people worked at the hotel switchboard. I was supposed to have worked there for three months. Before three days were up the guys there started to complain, 'Please, for mercy's sake, get this fellow out of here or we'll all walk out.' People envy a capable man everywhere. They went to my father-in-law and said, 'It's unbelievable. He knows everything. There's nothing we can teach him. He shouldn't waste his time for nothing.' They took me out of there and made me a waiter. I was supposed to have worked as a waiter for six months. Before six days were up, the waiters in the hotel rebelled: 'Either he goes or we do!'"

"And why? 'It's a shame for him to waste his time. It's incredible but he knows everything.' So they made me head waiter. There were thirty head waiters in the hotel. Before the second day was up the head waiters said, 'Either you get him out of here or we'll strike.' The same jealousy everywhere. Look here!"

"I'm sorry."

"You don't know who I am."

"I know who you are, Muammer."

"Well, if you had said you didn't know me...Then they made me the assistant manager of the hotel. My father-in-law could only stand it for one week. He went to the board of executives of the company that owned the hotel and said, 'Either him or me'. The board called me in. 'You know everything. You've finished your training,' they said. I said, 'I'm no fool. You can't finish your training in fifteen days. I'm not going anywhere.'

Then the chairman of the board said, 'Sir, please leave. If you don't, we'll not only have to leave the hotel but the country as well.'"

"Then I did something stupid. If I'd said 'I won't go anywhere,' those guys would have left the hotel to me and fled the country. 'I'll go,' I said, 'but you give me a testimonial.' 'If you'll only go,' they said, 'we'll give you a gilded testimonial.' 'I also want a letter of reference,' I said. 'We'll give you as many as you want,' they said. A member of the board then said, 'We'll give you as much money as you want, too.' 'I don't want any money,' I said. 'We owe you a lot. Since you came, we've learned to appreciate the people we had already working here. We're obligated to you. We'll give you whatever you want,' they said. My father-in-law said, 'You just go on back to your country. You find a place to build a hotel. I'll send your wife and however much money you want after you.' I left there and came over here. Four years went by. I write, my father-in-law doesn't answer. He hasn't sent me my wife or my money. Look here, here is my hotel management diploma. Here is the certificate showing that I'm a first class expert in hotel management. These are my letters of reference. They need hotels nowadays in this country. Everybody's getting in on the act, whether they know anything about it or not, but they don't appreciate quality or specialization. What's happened to me is a shame. Whatever official body I applied to brushed me off. Then I saw Rifat. Rifat sent me to see you. 'He knows people,' he said.

"What Rifat is that?"

"Rifat the Camel."

"I don't know who that is."

"Come on, didn't we all go to Galatasaray High School?"

"What do you mean, Galatasaray? I never went to Galatasaray."

I can't explain what happened after that. The neighbors came and saved me from him.

As he was going, he said, "You think you fooled me, do you?

I knew you didn't know me all the time. Damn it all, since you didn't know who I was, why did you try to pump a man you didn't know for secrets?"

Clinkity Clank

("Paldır Küldür" from *Hoptirinam*, 1960)

There is another unknown world besides this world which we know. Of that other unknown world with its six continents, there is a seventh continent also, unknown to those who live in the other six continents and in that continent there is an unknown country. So it was that these unknown men of the unknown world of the unknown country of the unknown continent had lived all to themselves since an unknown time.

One day a group of men from the known world went to that unknown country in an unknown continent in the unknown world. They spoke thus to the men who lived there:

"Oh unknown men, living since an unknown time in an unknown country in an unknown continent in an unknown world. We are the known men, living since a known time in a known country in a known continent in the known world. We see that you are very backward. We are very surprised that you are so backward."

The unknown men in the unknown country in the unknown continent in the unknown world were very angry at these words and said, "No, our country is not backward."

The men who had come from the known world said, "How could anyone tell that you weren't backward?"

The people from the known world said, "People fished five thousand years ago."

The unknown men said, "But we raise cattle. We have herds of cattle and we raise cows. We milk them and we make yoghurt."

The known men said, "People did that four thousand years ago."

The unknown men of the unknown world said, "But we practice agriculture. We sow and reap and we grow crops and farm."

The men from the known world said, "What you are talking about has been done for three thousand years."

The men from the unknown world said, "We raise cotton and we raise tobacco and we plant beets and we gather hazelnuts."

The known men said, "All these are things that have been going on for two thousand years."

It was then that the unknown people from the unknown country on the unknown continent of the unknown world were seized with consternation and they asked one another, "Are we really a backward, undeveloped country?"

They answered their own question themselves, "It's apparent that we are."

They asked the men from the known world, "What can we do to become developed? What do we have to do to develop?"

The known men from the known country on the known continent in the known world said, "Come, take a look at our country. You must do whatever we have done. See how we have developed by doing such things."

They thought this made sense. The unknown men from the unknown country in the unknown continent in the unknown world went to the known country in the known continent in the known world and learned through careful inspection what the known men did there. Then they went back to their own country.

The ones that got back first said, "We have caught on. They have machines."

The ones who came next said, "We have found out why they have progressed. They have machines."

The people coming from the known world all said: "Machines!"

"We have to make a machine so that we can progress."

"If we don't make a machine, we won't progress."

When they had all agreed on this, they said, "Then let's make a machine.

They sent heralds out through the whole country and had them shout,

"Let everyone who has seen machines in the known world and everyone who knows how to make machines come forward. We are going to make a machine in our country."

Everyone in the country who had seen a machine came together.

They told them, "Anything you desire is at your disposal and whatever you require is ready. All that matters is that you make a machine and that the country progress."

They started to make a machine. They worked and they worked and after working for years, the people who had made the machine examined the machine they had made from afar, and from nearby and from one side and from in front and from behind and from on top and they asked one another, "Do you suppose it's alright?"

The people who had seen machines in the known country in the known continent in the known world said, "Yes indeed, it's just like the machines over there."

Then they announced throughout the whole country, "The machine has been made. On such and such a day there will be an opening ceremony. Everyone is to come and see the machine we made."

There was wild excitement. Everyone came to look at the machine. One of the important people in the country said, "Now that we have made our machine we are going to progress."

Someone who had seen machines in the known world said,

"This is a machine, as far as machines go, but it seems to me that there is something missing about it. As I recollect, the machines I saw in the known country of the known world had wheels. This doesn't have any wheels."

"Oh yes," they said, "that's right. The machines we saw had wheels. This doesn't. Let's make wheels for it right away."

At this command the workers and the master craftsmen started to work. The made a bunch of wheels and fitted them here and there on the machine they had set up but they found the wheels too few and added still more to them. In this way the machine became something enormous.

They started it working again. They made big and small spindles and stuck them here and there on the machine any place they found an empty spot. As the pivots were added to the machine over the years the machine got so big that it could no longer fit in the city where it had been set up. When this was completed, guns were fired and it was proclaimed that the machine had been completed. The people of the country went to see the machine and rejoice. One of the important people said, "Aha, this is what a machine should be like. And we have made a very big machine besides."

Another said, "The machine is fine as far as it goes but it seems to me that these machine are missing something. Didn't the machines we saw have rollers?"

"Oh yes", the others said. "You remember correctly. We almost made machines without rollers and we would have waited to progress in vain. Let's make rollers for our machines right away."

They started making rollers. They made rollers for years and stuck them on the machines. The machine grew and grew until it covered a third of the country so that in the end it had become a super big machine: all who saw it said, "Oh my, how fine!"

The old and young, sick and well, children and grownups of that country came to see the machine.

The important people of the country said, "Marvelous!

Really...This is what a machine should be like."

But one in their midst said, "I wonder if I remember correctly but, as I recall, the machines we saw had things like boilers and furnaces."

One of the important people said, "That's it. I have been thinking all the time that this machine was missing something. I wondered what it could be. That's perfectly right, it needs boilers and furnaces. You can't make a machine without boilers and furnaces. Let's make some boilers and furnaces and crucibles for it immediately."

"Right away" they said and went to work. They made boilers and they made furnaces. After working for years and filling every part of the machine with boilers and furnaces they announced to the leaders, "There's no place left to stick any more boilers or furnaces. It must be finished."

Once more the people assembled, rejoicing. The important people of the country who had arrived amidst applause said, when they saw the machine, "Aha, this is what we call a machine. Now there is no reason left for us not to progress. The machine is finished."

A bystander said "Don't you think there's something missing in this machine? The machines we saw had something called belts. Where are the belts on this thing?"

"God bless you," the others who heard this said. "Why we were about to make a machine without any belts. You see what was happening. Make some belts and put them on the machine immediately."

They worked for years and made belts, big and small, and attached them to the machine. But the machine had grown so big, it had grown so much that it covered half the country.

When the belts had been attached a celebration never before seen took place throughout the country. They came to see the machine to the sound of horns and drums. When the important people in the country saw the machine, they said, "Glory be! We finally finished this machine. Now we are going to progress, have no fear."

But again one of them came forward and said, "I don't remember exactly but the machines we saw had something else, it seems to me. Ah, now I remember, they were horns, horns. Where are the horns on this machine? You can't have a machine without horns. All the machines we saw had horns."

The others shouted, "Thank goodness for your advice. How could we have forgotten. Horns, of course, horns. You can't have a machine without horns. Here, we were about to forget and all our trouble would have been for nothing. Come on, let's make horns for the machine."

They set to work and they worked for years and they stuck horns wherever they found an empty spot on the machine. As they kept on adding the horns, the machine grew so big that it almost covered the whole country.

The people came running in holiday glee to see the machine. The important people looked and looked at the machine and said, "Now it's finished. It doesn't lack anything. At last we've made the machine. Now we'll progress."

Just about then, one of them said, "It seems to me that there is still something missing."

The other important people said, "That can't be! The machine is so big that it can hardly fit inside the whole country. What could a machine like that be missing? Don't go getting us confused for no reason."

The opposition said, "We don't care what you may say. There's something missing in this machine. Didn't the machines we saw go 'clinkity clank', 'clinkity clank'? The rollers went round, the wheels turned, the gears intermeshed, the belts ran along, whirring, the boilers bubbled, the furnace burned, the spindles went in and out, the cranks rose and fell and there was a continual commotion whereas this machine of ours doesn't let out a peep."

The others thought and thought and then they said, "That's very true. The machines we saw let out 'clinkity clank' noises. The wheels and belts and flywheels turned ceaselessly. So we've made this machine for all that it is worth but now we have to worry about the racket. Well, come on then. Let's do that too. Let's get it over with."

They worked for years, they struggled and they lit furnaces and boiled the water in boilers. They attached spindles to rollers and rollers to gears and gears to cranks and cranks to belts and belts to horns and horns to bolts. At the end of all this striving, the wheels started to turn, the spindles to operate, the flywheels to turn, the belts to work, the horns to toot, the rollers to roll and the bolts to clunk. There was such a racket that heaven and earth began to groan with the noise. Everybody who heard the racket came running to see the machine, their eyes brimming with tears of joy. All the people in the country gathered around the machine. They started to celebrate.

The important people of the country, puffed up with their success, asked one another, "Take a good look. Can you think of anything else? For goodness sake, let's not leave anything out of the machine."

Nobody could think of anything missing. It was just exactly like a machine.

"Perfect," they said. "It has everything and more. If it were missing something, would it make all that clanking? Our machine is even bigger than theirs. Listen to the noise and commotion. What a lot of noise our machine makes!"

The others said, "Yes, we made a machine at last and now we are going to progress. Let's keep this machine working continuously from now on so that we can progress.

They threw kindling ceaselessly into the machine's furnace. The furnace burned on without stopping and the machine kept on working.

Because they progressed a little more everyday as the machine worked, they were happy but because this huge machine covered most of their country they no longer could raise livestock or sow seeds or till the soil or raise crops.

Regardless, they rejoiced, saying, "We have our machine now. Now we are going to progress."

Once more, one day the known men from the known country in the known continent in the known world came to the unknown country in the unknown continent in the unknown world and they saw the unknown people.

They asked them, "What is this deafening clatter?"

And they told them, "Why, it's a machine. It's the machine we have made. As the machine is working, we too are advancing."

The men from the known world said, "What do you mean, advancing? You are worse off now than you were before. What kind of a machine is this anyway?"

The men from the unknown world said, "This is exactly like your machines. In fact, it's bigger than your machines. It has horns and gears. It has wheels and bolts. It has a boiler and a furnace and flywheels. It has rollers and everything else. And it even works."

The known men from the known country in the known continent in the known world said, "Well and good, but what does this machine make? What is it good for? What does it produce?"

The unknown men from the unknown country in the unknown continent in the unknown world asked in amazement, "Oh my, was this machine supposed to make something? Was it supposed to produce something?"

"Why did you make a machine that doesn't produce anything? What good is it?"

The unknown men from the unknown country said, "Right you are. We made the machine. Now let's make the machine make something for us."

Later however, they said to themselves, "It makes noise doesn't it? That's enough for us. Listen: 'clinkity clank, clinkity clank'."

A Pair of Glasses

("Gözüne Gözlük" from *Gözüne Gözlük*,1960)

I needed a medical report. At the age of twenty-four, I thought that my whole future would depend on that medical report. All the tests showed me to be in good health. The only thing left was my eye examination. Because I was so confident of my eyes, I left that till last.

After the eye test, the doctor said, "I'm going to put in your report that you're one dioptric myopic and I'm writing you a prescription for glasses."

The world suddenly seemed grey and dreary. I thought, with my inexperience at that age, that if my eyes hadn't turned out to be bad, and thus my bright future hadn't been suddenly darkened, I would have turned into something completely different from what I was: into a great man. What, for example? Well, a captain on a ferryboat or a department head in some office.

Before this happened, I could see a fly on the tail of a black cow at five hundred paces, now I couldn't read the print in the newspaper even if I held it under my nose.

I told everybody who asked me, "I'm myopic."

"You can't be myopic," they said.

"Why?"

"Myopic people can't see in the distance and you can't see what's nearby."

I had learned in school that myopic people can't see what's far away but I had forgotten that. After others had straightened me out on the matter, I started reading newspapers and books again but I could not see a wall three feet away. I wanted to buy some glasses but I had lost the prescription. I had my eyes checked by another doctor.

The doctor said, "There's nothing wrong with your eyes."

"How can that be? Last month I was one dioptric myopic."

The doctor got angry. He said, "Whoever said that was just plain dumb."

Because I was of the same opinion, I started to see much better than before. I didn't wear any glasses until I was forty-five. Seven or eight months earlier a friend who came to the house had asked, "Why don't you wear glasses?"

"Why should I?"

"At your age, you have to. If you don't start wearing glasses now, later on your eyes will go completely bad and you won't be able to see anything."

My friend left and a fog settled over my vision. I couldn't see anything, close or distant. By the way, I have to tell my secret quirk. I have always secretly wanted two things in life. One was to lose my hair and have a receding hairline and the other was to wear glasses. These two things show a man to be an intellectual. If a butcher boy were to lose his hair and put on glasses, you could make him an assistant professor at the university and nobody would know the difference.

Not even one of my wishes came true, not that anything that I had ever wished for had actually happened. My hair got thicker every day, but at least I could wear the glasses and people would think I was an educated man.

I went to an eye doctor. He examined me.

"One seventy-five dioptric myopic," he said.

So the doctor who examined me twenty years before was

right after all! The dioptric had increased from that time and now it was seventy-five.

I got a pair of glasses made according to his prescription. As soon as I put those glasses on, my head started to spin, I felt sick at my stomach and I started, pardon the expression, vomiting all over the place. I threw up everything I had inside me as if I were in a boat on a rough sea. I would take my glasses off and I couldn't see anything. When I put them on, not only could I not see anything but I vomited. If I put them on, I had one sort of trouble and if I didn't, I had another. It was a pain.

A friend felt sorry for me. He said, "Let me recommend you a really good eye doctor. You go to him."

I went. The doctor first examined me, then he looked at the glasses.

"What monkey prescribed you these glasses? You're not myopic."

"What am I then?"

"Hypermyopic, two dioptrics hypermyopic."

I had known there had been something wrong. If somebody could think that a hypermyopic was myopic, wouldn't that cause the trouble?

I got another pair of glasses according to this prescription. These glasses didn't make me vomit and they didn't make me sick to my stomach, however they did make me cry. The instant I put them on, tears burst from my eyes. I would sob my heart out. When I cried, a sadness oppressed me and I would weep floods. The only thing these glasses were good for was to wear at funerals. My eyes were bloodshot from weeping.

A good friend said, "Look here, you're going to go blind. Go to a government hospital. A great big government hospital is different from a private doctor's office."

The eye doctor at the hospital was even a professor. Yes indeed, a clinic is something else. There was every kind of instrument and it all shone and glittered.

The professor examined my eyes. I told him what had happened to me.

"One eye is myopic and the other is hypermyopic," I said.

The professor was enraged. "That son of a this and that," he shouted. "Your eyes aren't either myopic or hypermyopic. You're astigmatic."

I had another pair of glasses made according to the professor's prescription. These glasses were really good. I could see everything with them. The only thing was, nothing was where it should have been. The world had moved away and left me behind. The wall of the room where I had lived for ten years had moved back thirty meters. I couldn't even shake a friend's hand. I would want to write something, the paper underneath my hand looked as if it were two meters away. It was something like looking through the wrong end of a pair of binoculars. Everything was far away and tiny. People looked like lentil beans. Well, maybe I could learn to like this and start feeling important. Everything was little and far away. Oh, this was great! It was all fine except I couldn't eat. When I sat at the table, the plate looked twenty meters away. I would stick my nose in the hot soup and I would stretch my spoon out to a soup dish that looked as though it were two meters away. I couldn't eat, drink or walk around.

They led me by the arm to another eye doctor. This doctor had studied in America. They claimed that he had implanted a wolf's eyes in a mole.

After a tremendously long examination, he said, "What blankity blank gave you these glasses? My God, what a stupid bum! And these guys call themselves doctors? If you file a complaint, they'll take his license away."

"I'll leave his punishment to God," I said.

"Your right eye is one and a half and your left eye is two dioptrics myopic."

I bought a new pair of glasses. Now, everything looked double. There are seven people at my house and they looked like fourteen. At first I didn't pay any attention because I said to myself, "People look very much like one another and these people must have been created double." Even if people do look alike, do they look that much alike? Well, other people are one thing but what about me myself? When I looked at my feet, I had four. I had ten fingers on just one hand. I was ready to go crazy.

I went to another eye doctor. This one had studied in Germany. "What blankity blank blank gave you these glasses?" he said.

"What is the matter with them?"

"What do you think? They are wrong."

My left eye was three dioptrics myopic astigmatic and my right eye was two and a half dioptrics hypermetropic.

After I had put on the glasses he gave me, I couldn't see anything, day or night. Everything was pitch black. They led me to another doctor.

The man laughed, "What blankity blank blank blank wrote this prescription? There is nothing wrong with your eyes. They are perfectly normal."

"I can't see anything. Everything is black."

"That's just because you are suffering from night blindness."

Pills, shots, vitamins and a pair of new glasses. When I put these glasses on, everything in the distance looked as though it were right under my nose. When I stepped out from the pier to get into the ferry, I almost fell in the sea. Before the ferry would moor at the pier, I would be boarding it.

There wasn't an eye doctor left that I hadn't visited. If one said that my right eye was myopic and my left eye was hypermetropic, the other one said just the opposite. One said I was astigmatic and another that I had a cataract. The glasses that the one who said I had cataracts gave me, made me see green. Then the doctor said, "He's suffering from color blindness".

That is, thanks to the glasses, I saw things in as many shapes and colors as one could see, whether from a distance or from nearby. The last glasses I put on made everything look as though it were far below me. The world had sunk 40 or 50 centimeters below my feet. When I walked down a level road, I felt as though I were walking down a stairway. I started walking "flopity-flop" like a camel. That was why, when I was going down the steps to the Bridge, I tried to take a step because the stair under my foot looked a meter lower than it was and I fell, rolling all the way to the bottom.

My glasses had fallen off. I couldn't see anything without glasses. It was as though I were surrounded by a mist. They helped me up off the ground.

"But where are my glasses?" I said.

They found my glasses and I put them on. My God, I don't ever remember having seen so well in my life before. Everything was where it was supposed to be, clear, beautiful. I looked to see whether I had put on somebody else's glasses by mistake. No, these were my own, thick, black-framed glasses. I can't tell you how happy I was. At last I was free from eye doctors. I could read the smallest print in the newspapers and see the name on the ferryboat from far away.

In that same good mood, I got home.

My wife asked, "What happened to the lenses in your glasses?"

"What do you mean?"

I took my glasses off. I could put my finger all the way through the frame of the glasses. No, there was no glass in the glasses. It must have broken when I fell down the steps.

Ever since that day I have seen very well without glasses.

We Humans

("Biz İnsanlar" from *Hoptirinam*, 1960)

Very long ago, very recently, from before, from behind, from the other side, from this side, from yesterday, from tomorrow and both before I was born and after I had died there was a town on the face of the earth and there was a house amongst the houses of that town. This town of which I speak exists in whatever century and in whatever country the readers, tellers and listeners to this story may live. It was built in that country. Whatever language the readers speak who have read this story before me and who will read it after me is the language they spoke in that town.

It all happened at eight o'clock in the morning when the man of the house awoke. The man woke up in his bed, rubbed his eyes and stretched. He looked and there was another head, a frightful one, right on the pillow where his head lay. The head was neither that of man nor animal. It was the head of a monster, never yet seen nor heard of. Huge buffalo eyes were sunk into its forehead. It puffed from its swine snout which opened and closed like a bellows. Its ears were the ears of a donkey. An eagle's claw swelled up a hundred fold and a dog's tail protruded from under the quilt.

But the man had gotten into the bed with his wife the night

89

before. The bed which they had shared for thirty years he had shared again the night before with his wife.

When the man opened his eyes and saw that a frightful monster lay in his bosom, he opened his arms wide and throwing himself against the wall, he shouted at the top of his voice. The waking monster started at the sound of his cry.

"What is the matter with you, dear?" it asked.

The monster could talk like a human being. And its voice was the voice of his wife. Only his wife's voice was softer than ever, sweeter, much more lovely.

The man, when he heard the monster speaking in his wife's voice, leapt out of the bed in his underclothes. Running to a corner of the room, he crouched down. The monster got out of bed too, putting on a pink jersey slip. It wasn't a monster so much as a giantess. It threw its breasts over either shoulder like empty flour bags. Its hair looked like chimney brooms, like witches' hair.

It asked, stretching out its right claw towards the man who was trembling with fear, "What is the matter with you, dear? What is the matter?"

Ah, what a sweet, moving voice this giantess had! The man covered his face with both his hands in order not to see the giantess and started screaming, scream after scream. Suddenly the bedroom door opened. Three strange creatures came in. They resembled three boa constrictors walking on two human legs. Their skin was all scales. But these things weren't all snakes. They had long furry tails. One of them had long flaxen hair that tumbled down onto its shoulders.

The man screamed "Help!" at the top of his voice, his eyes popping out of their sockets when he saw these three strange creatures.

The flaxen-haired one went towards the man, saying, "Daddy, Daddy!"

Then the three of them cuddled up to the man, saying "Dad, Daddy, what's the matter?"

The man was frightened and baffled. The three strange creatures who were mixtures of snakes, mules and humans, were talking to him in the voices of his children.

The man threw himself towards the door, screaming "Mammaaa!"

He had a mother who was about eighty years old. His mother's voice came from the inner room, "What's the matter, my son?"

When the man opened the door from which the voice came he almost fell down in a faint. Inside was a creature with a human face and the body of a mangy cow, covered in sores.

"What is it, my son?"

The thing with the cow's body whose mouth opened from the nape of its neck and whose nose was set in the middle of its forehead, spoke exactly in his mother's voice.

The man ran and put on his clothes. While he was dressing as fast as he could, the giantess, the creatures who looked like three snakes and the cow-like thing surrounded him and asked him, "Tell us, dearest? What is the matter?"

The one who was dressed as a giantess asked, "Why do you look at us so afraid?"

The snake mutant with the flaxen hair asked, "Daddy, why are you shaking?"

The man shouted, "Get away from me!"

He barely managed to throw himself into the street. But what should he see but the street was filled with strange creatures that he had never seen before that day? They were neither exactly animals nor men. They were creatures with rhinoceros heads set on elephant bodies and camel bodies with orangutan faces. There were plodding, hopping frogs with men's heads, swollen up as big as cows. The streets were full of these things. If all the zoos on earth had been emptied, it still couldn't have turned out like this because these weren't even animals.

The man started to run through the streets with his hands on his head in a great panic but there was no way that he could save himself from these disgusting, frightful creatures. He ran and he ran until he was winded. He ran up the stairs of the office where he worked. Even his office was filled with these disgusting, strange creatures. He ran into his office. He went to his desk and sat in his chair. He rang the buzzer to call the office messenger.

A turkey with a dog's head on two human feet came in and said, "What can I do for you, sir?"

The man screamed, "I'm going crazy! I'm going crazy!"

The turkey-like creature who had come in, asked him, "Why is that, sir? Is there something that is irritating you?"

The voice was the voice which he knew very well of the customary office messenger.

Closing his eyes in order not to have to look at him, he said, "Quick, call me Miss F."

"Yes, sir."

Miss F was the office typist whom the man loved madly. She was a girl of surpassing beauty. In a little while the door opened.

In came a seal with its hide all slick but with four dog's feet and with a huge tail longer than that of a snake's behind.

When the man saw this, he screamed, covering his face with his hands, "Who are you?"

The seal-like creature said, "You sent for me."

The man, who had turned crazy, rushed out of the door and into the General Director's office. Another disgusting monster was sitting at the desk.

He came back out, hopeless.

"Is it possible that I'm dreaming? Am I dreaming? Am I asleep?" he muttered to himself.

He ran into the street. There again were those monsters, those strange creatures, gigantic spiders, centipedes as big as elephants, scorpions with men's heads, crocodiles walking on the feet of geese...

The man ran through the streets, crying "Save me. Save me" and throwing himself here and there in a fit. He ran and ran and screamed and screamed.

All the strange creatures who saw him running and screaming like that, chased after him. They started to chase the man in order to catch him. The man kept running away. A hyena jumped out in front of him but the man dodged it in order not to be caught and kept on running. A strange-looking swine tripped him up but the man leapt up from where he had fallen and kept on running.

He kept on screaming, "Help, save me!"

This chase went on for hours through the streets of the town. Finally the man collapsed in a ditch in an alleyway.

The man-animal mutant monsters who stood all around him murmured, "What a shame, the poor man has gone crazy."

They bound the man's hands and feet firmly with ropes. They cuffed his wrists together and chained his feet and brought him to a big building in a vehicle. On the door was written "Hospital for Mental Diseases". They took the man in and put him into a room on the door of which was written "Chief Doctor".

The man was moaning, "Save me. Isn't there a human being here? Save me."

A creature with a awful face, camel hooves and the body of a crab and wearing a doctor's smock, came in and said, "Let him loose!"

They freed the man from his ropes and chains. The man turned his back to the people in the room and dropped his head to his knees. The white smocked creature asked him in a gentle voice, "What is the matter with you?"

The man who was crouched down, said, without raising his head from his knees, "Nothing is the matter with me."

"Why won't you look at me?"

The man explained what had happened to him ever since he had opened his eyes that morning, then he moaned, "Where are human beings? Where are human beings? I want to see a human."

A sound resembling a laugh came from the white smocked thing.

"I see. I see," it said. "I will give you a quick treatment."

Having said this, he turned to a huge turtle who was standing beside him and said, "Young lady, bring us the ME mirror."

Two creatures, crosses between huge pigs and hyenas, brought in a big mirror. There in the mirror was an image more terrifying and disgusting than anything that he had seen since he had opened his eyes that morning. It was the face of a mutilated man, blood and pus dripping from the wounds. The teeth were long and two of them hung down below his chin. He had donkey's ears, popping eyes as big as saucers and horns growing out of the top of his head. He was a poisonous green lizard with a scaly skin and a big body.

The man screamed in terror at the disgusting and frightful image he saw and then he fell down in a faint.

After lying in a faint for a while, he opened his eyes and asked in a weak voice, "Where am I?"

The white smocked doctor said, "You are here in the hospital. How are you? Are you alright?"

The man said, smiling, "Thank you, doctor. I am very well."

The doctor said, "From now on, look into yourself to find whatever you need."

At the doctor's side were two lovely female assistants. The man left after thanking them. In the streets were the usual sort of people. He worked in his office until evening. Then he went home...

He said to his wife, "How are you, my dear?"

His wife said, "Good morning. You slept a long time this morning. Your breakfast is ready. We are waiting for you."

The man washed up, after getting out of bed, then he kissed his children.

He heard a voice from inside, "How are you, my son?"

The man answered, "Very well, mother. I hope you're well too."

One Madman for One Hundred Liras

("Yüz Liraya Bir Deli" from *Yüz Liraya Bir Deli,* 1961)

From what the people call the "madhouse" and from what doctors, if they are in an official position, call the Mental Hospital, five madmen, pardon, five mental patients, escaped. The date on which the hospital personnel learned that the five mental patients were no longer in the hospital was accepted as the date on which the five patients ran away. In actual fact, in what month, on what day and at what time the five patients ran off will never be known.

When the incident was announced, both the personnel and the doctors were greatly alarmed because the escapees were the most deranged, aggressive patients who had already committed various crimes. There was even one among them who liked to start fires.

The Administrator telephoned the Governor's Office and the Directorate of Security. These dangerous mental patients must be arrested before they could cause some grievous mishap.

The Director on duty who talked with the Hospital Administrator on the phone, informed him that for the police to be able to arrest the madmen it would be necessary "for the hospital to officially petition in writing". Certainly it must to be thus. The Administrator knew this as well. But the madmen must be caught with "all haste". Allah only knew how many days it would take for an official document to get from the hospital to the office of the Directorate of Security. Would the Directorate of Security assume the responsibility for the damage that the madmen might cause in the mean time? Certainly, an official paper could be sent later on.

The Director on duty started to make notes on the piece of paper in front of him: "Date...hour...Today five madmen escaped. One of the madmen is wearing a striped hospital uniform."

"One of the runaways was a woman. Since the woman and one of the male patients had left behind the hospital uniforms they had on, they must have fled naked. The other two escapees fled in the stolen clothes of hospital personnel."

Over the telephone, the Security Director on duty said to the Hospital Administrator, "My dear sir, how can I catch five crazy people in this huge city? Don't they have any, you know, marks or signs?"

And the Administrator, losing his temper, said, "I told you, sir. One is wearing striped hospital clothes. Two of them are dressed as hospital attendants and two of them are naked."

"Well, if somebody is walking around town naked, that's an easy one...Don't these madmen have any other identifying signs?"

"Oh yes, they do. I'll pass the phone to the doctor for that department and he can tell you."

The Administrator gave the phone to the doctor at his side and the Director on duty gave the telephone receiver to a police official, saying, "Write down what the gentleman says."

The escapees from the hospital were schizophrenics. As regards the patients' identifying signs...they behaved abnormally. In short, any persons whose abnormal behavior made them suspect were to be caught and taken in for questioning.

The Ministry also took an interest in the runaway madmen, for whatever reason. The affair became more serious still. The madmen were dangerous, very dangerous...They must be arrested with all urgency.

A little while later, this order was transmitted by wireless and by telephone to the local security headquarters and from the security headquarters to the individual police stations by telephone,

"This is to inform you for reasons of urgency, with written order to follow: It has been learned from information given by the Hospital Administrator that five mental patients, one of them a woman, have escaped last night from the Mental Hospital and that these patients are extremely dangerous. The female patient and one of the males are naked and one of the others is wearing the striped hospital uniform, while two of the other patients are wearing the clothes of the hospital attendants. The Hospital Administrator has informed us that the five escapees behave abnormally. In order to apprehend these five mental patients who may create confusion and disorder in the city, as well as being a danger, you are requested herewith to arrest any persons exhibiting abnormal behavior and send them to the Mental Hospital for examination."

"Note: The Ministry has announced that it will pay the police personnel arresting any of these mental patients a cash reward of one hundred liras per arrest."

In one of the police stations which had received this order by telephone, the Captain called his police together.

"Is there anything you don't understand about the order?" he asked.

When the policemen didn't make a sound, thinking the order had been understood, he said, "Come on, friends, to work. We'll hold a search through our district. The order is clear, if you see anybody acting abnormally...Alright? One hundred liras a madman."

One of the policemen was muttering, "Let's go on the madman hunt, on the madman hunt..."

A policeman sitting at the desk said, "What a pain! If I wasn't on duty, I'd go and hunt crazy men too."

A security guard standing behind the policeman said, "Cap-

tain, if Allah ordains and I run across a madman and arrest
him, would a guard be paid a hundred liras too?"

The Captain said, "No difference. We're in this together."

A little while after they had started on this assignment, a
policeman came into the Captain's room.

"I caught one right off. I threw him in the detention cell and
I'm off to look for the others."

"That was fast! Where'd you catch him?"

"I was leaving the police station and he was right there, in
front of the door."

"How'd you know he was crazy?"

He started to answer, "Would anybody who wasn't crazy
walk in front of the police station" but he kept his mouth shut.

"You said 'abnormal'. This one was abnormal."

At that instant, another policeman came rejoicing into the
Captain's room. He said, holding the fingers of his right hand
together, "I found two mad men, *halis muhlis* mad they are."

"How do you know?"

"We-ell, one's called 'Halis' and the other's called 'Muhlis.' "

The Captain said, "Let's not lose any more time and write
the report right away."

The officer at the desk put a piece of paper in the typewriter.

"Write this, 'This is to inform you that policeman number
2876, attached to our precinct...' write your name, 'having
arrived after long and arduous research at the conclusion that
two abnormal acting persons were two of the five patients
escaped from the crazy house,' erase 'crazy house' and write
'Mental Hospital' . . . 'and in order to prevent any unfortunate
incidents, has taken the same into custody and to prevent
their escape has placed our fellow citizen mental patients in
the detention cell to be dispatched to the Mental Hospital.'
That sentence is probably incorrect."

The security guard came joyfully into the Captain's room,
saying, "I got good news."

The guard was pushing two half naked men before him,

"Thank the Lord, I got two hundred liras in my pocket."

The Captain said, "What do you mean, two hundred liras?"

"Captain, thanks to you, I caught two mad men and them's the rarest kind, naked madmen."

"These guys aren't naked."

"Well, you could call them naked but if you like I can take them inside there and strip them down to buff... I'll stick them in the detention cell and go out and get some others. Have a look. It's just boiling with madmen out there."

The police stations informed the Directorate of Security that so far nine people had been observed acting abnormally and had been arrested on suspicion of being mad. This situation amazed the concerned parties and they inquired from the Mental Hospital by phone:

"Since review of our records shows that the number of persons observed to be acting abnormally and to have been arrested is now at nine persons, we request your hospital urgently to notify us of the actual number of madmen having escaped from you."

A count of the crazy people in the hospital once more showed that, with the exception of the personnel on leave, only five mental patients were missing. Before these results had been communicated, the number of persons who had been observed acting abnormally and arrested in the city, had risen to twenty-six. As the number of persons arrested and sent to the hospital in the effort to catch the five runaway mental patients grew, the Hospital Administrator shouted at the top of his voice:

"No! No! Stop! This place is turning into a crazy house. I can't control my own patients. Where am I going to put these? What am I going to do?"

The Hospital Administrator sent this message to the office of the Director of Security:

"However much according to the records compiled in the police stations as a result of the efforts of our selfless police force, you have succeeded in arresting twenty-six abnormal-

acting persons, in order to avoid substituting other individuals in the place of the five mental patient escapees and to preclude errors, it is essential that these twenty-six persons be examined by specialists in order that only the real escaped mental patients be institutionalized in our hospital. Unfortunately, at the same time, neither the patient escaping in hospital uniform nor the two naked escapees are among those who have been delivered to our hospital."

This communication must have just been received from the Hospital administration because it was revealed that over one hundred abnormal-appearing people had been apprehended by the police. While it was understood both from their own confessions and from the testimony of witnesses that they had engaged in abnormal behavior, a large number of these persons had been arrested on complaints from members of their families, relatives and neighbors concerning their craziness. Just as there were women who denounced their husbands as crazy, there were also husbands who denounced their wives as being mad.

At this point the ones who created complete confusion were those who appeared at the police stations of their own free will saying, "We're crazy". Some of them submitted petitions like this: *"I have escaped from the Mental Hospital. I heard I was being searched for. I am sorry that I ran away. Because I have finally understood the truth and am sorry at having run away, I hereby request that I be reaccepted by the Mental Hospital."*

Things became completely confused. A new problem emerged. Since those persons who had come of their own free will, saying "We are crazy" had not been arrested by the police, it meant that the hundred liras a head reward that had been promised for every madman that was arrested would not be paid out for these people. For this reason, the police didn't believe those persons who ran to the police stations with petitions in their hands, saying "We are crazy". Such a citizen would be chased for a kilometer from the station, cut off and caught by the policeman on duty at the station and, since this man was a madman whom he had caught, he would deliver him to the Mental Hospital together with a report bearing his badge number.

But here was the difficulty: Were there any of the escapees from the Mental Hospital amongst the people that had been caught?

According to the latest information obtained from the Hospital administration, things had gone completely amuck:

"As the result of examinations of those persons observed to be behaving abnormally and sent to our hospital, all have been diagnosed to be suffering from mental and nervous diseases and have been institutionalized in our hospital. However it has not been possible to assertain whether any of the five patients who have escaped were amongst those arrested by our selfless and earnest police force."

The police arrested the madmen who had escaped naked on the bathing beaches. Quite a few people were caught in abnormal positions during the raids on the beaches. Although quite a few of these declared that that they were not crazy and that they had been arrested naked in the beach's changing cabins while they were taking their underwear off and putting their swim suits on or taking their swim suits off but with their underwear on, nothing they said was taken into account with the idea that a madman never acknowledges his madness.

In the raids made on the hotels, during which the hotel rooms were scrutinized through the keyhole and a good number of people, whether in the room or in bed were seen engaging in abnormal behavior, a large number of people in striped pijamas were caught. And especially in the bordellos, the people in striped pijamas who were observed in abnormal postures had gone so far in their insanity as to assail the fervent fellow citizens who gathered there.

Although the policemen who had hunted the madmen demanded their hundred liras a madman cash reward that had been advertised, submitting petitions, since it could not be determined whether or not the five real madmen who had determined whether or not the five real madmen who had escaped from the hospital were amongst those arrested, it was announced that the rewards would not be distributed until a definite conclusion could be reached.

After this discouraging response, the number of madmen arrested for having been seen to engage in abnormal behavior, decreased day by day. While the madman hunt had caught nine people on the first day and twenty-six on the second day and while on the following days it had increased with even more people being arrested, as soon as the money reward was dropped, the number fell off, from day to day. Things cooled off considerably. Now the police didn't observe anybody in the city engaging in abnormal behavior.

Even though it was not clear whether the five escapee madmen had ever been caught or not, since nobody was observed to engage in abnormal behavior any longer, it was apparent that the great city had been freed of madmen. On a day when this was still thought to be so, the police officers were having this conversation amongst themselves in one of the neighborhood police stations:

"You can't win serving this country of ours, my friend. . ."

The First Woman Ever to Understand Me

("Beni Anlayan İlk Kadın" from *Sosyalizm Geliyor Savulun,* 1965)

I had been invited that evening to the home of a former cabinet minister. I'd like to note discreetly at this point that while they are in office, these people called ministers, be they friends or not, don't invite me to come and see them, either at their offices or homes, nor do they visit me at my house or anywhere else but after they have fallen from office, I say this with gratitude, there are some of them who remember me.

When I went to the villa of his honor the Ex-Minister, set on a lush green hill lapped by the calm blue waters of the Sea of Marmara, the wide reception room, the terrace and the gardens were filled with guests holding glasses of drinks in their hands, laughing and talking to one another. The moon had risen early and sea and trees were bathed in moonlight.

There is no point in trying to hide it: everybody knows my shyness and slowness. I slunk into the darkness of the garden without being seen and without mixing with the crowd that was emitting male and female bursts of laughter. I sat down in one of the three iron chairs at the foot of a big pine tree. A few colored electric lights hanging from the branches of the tree did nothing except spoil the beauty of the moonlit night.

On my way to the Ex-Minister's house, I had stopped in on a friend and had seen a book in his library that I had been looking for for ages and hadn't been able to find. I had asked him if I might borrow it to read for a few days. I had the book with me. It wouldn't have been proper to have showed up at the Minister's evening invitation with a book. I don't like those people who are never without a book under their arms to show people that they are intellectuals, people who don't even go to the toilet without a book. I don't know what they would say about me if they saw me here with a book. It was a thick volume and wouldn't go into my pocket. I set the book on the iron table in front of me. When the silly laughter and the noisy conversation inside died down in a little, I would go inside and see my friend the Ex-Minister.

A man was coming towards me in the darkness. The man who came up to me bore a tray with glasses of drinks on it. The waiter, valet, servant or whatever he may have been, had seen me from afar and held out the tray to me. In that semi-darkness, I took a glass of what I thought was tomato juice. As soon as I had poured the ice-cold tomato juice down my throat, which I did because I was very thirsty in the hot weather, my insides caught on fire. Flames shot from my eyes. It was some strong drink I had never before tasted. I left the glass on top of the table.

I first heard the rustling of the dry grass and then approaching footsteps. The footsteps came nearer, moved away and then came back and wandered around me. I could discern in the twilight that it was a woman. A woman circling about me made me nervous. Ever since I can remember, I have been timid of women, especially beautiful ones. It always seemed to me that they made sly fun of me. Maybe my awkwardness comes from my first and last declaration of love, made twenty-five years before. She was a university student. One day I went with her to the island of Büyükada. Perhaps a thousand times I made up my mind to confess my love to her and every time I made the girl laugh at me with every sort of nonsense besides love but that day my decision was firm. We climbed down to the seashore from the high rocks and sat down side by side on a rock half in the sea. After swallowing for a while, I started to pour out my feelings. While I spoke, I couldn't look at the girl on my right at all. I kept looking straight ahead and trained my eyes on the far horizon. I kept on murmuring the most beautiful words of love I could manage. I didn't time how long I talked with a watch but the shadow of the hill that loomed over us moved away and the sun warmed us, then, once more, the shadows returned. Since it doesn't matter, really, I'll tell the girl's name: Handan...

I would stop every so often so Handan might answer my verbal love making. But she, it must have been because of her shyness, never made a sound. I went on without ever turning my head in her direction. The sun was sinking into the sea, on the horizon. I stopped speaking. Even my bottom had grown numb from sitting on the hard rock. Interpreting Handan's silence as her acceptance of my love and with a masculine audacity that came into my life at that moment I wanted to put my arms around Handan's waist, her shoulders or wherever my hand might land but I could by no means turn my head in her direction. I slung my right arm out but when I did, I found myself in free space, rolling head over heels from the top of the rock into the sea. If the lower part of my body hadn't grown completely numb, this accident would never have befallen me. But worst of all, while I was thrusting out my right arm, I was about to say,

"Handan! Now you say something, Handan! Speak, Handan! Answer me, Handan!"

Because I had already started to speak, quite naturally, I couldn't hold myself back and kept on saying the words after I was in the water,

"Handan! Answer me, Handan!" I moaned.

A saucy burst of laughter which resounded through the hills answered these moans. I raised my head from the sea and saw that Handan was laughing at me in resounding peels from the top of a pine tree on top of the high cliff behind me. My behind and my legs had gotten so numb that I just couldn't stand up and straighten myself out in the water in which I was struggling. Handan, jumping from rock to rock, reached my side and grabbing me by the hand, pulled me to my feet. But she laughed so hard with tears flowing from her eyes, that she rolled on the pebbles.

"What happened? Did you just fall off like that or did you fall asleep on top of that rock?" she said.

This meant that she must have got up and left a long time since and that I must have been muttering about love all to myself.

Handan was holding her sides, saying, "Did you hurt yourself?"

I couldn't say a single word. We got on the steamer. We parted at the Bridge.

I have been shy of women since that day and that is the reason I have never married.

I was about to move somewhere else to get away from the woman who kept wandering around me, when the woman came right up to me.

"You love solitude like all great men, Hasan Bey," she said.

I peered into her face to see who the woman who even knew my name was but I couldn't recognize her. Since I couldn't decide how to answer her, I said, "What, for instance, madam?"

Whenever I can't think how to answer somebody, I ask an absurd question like "What, for instance?", to gain time to pull myself together.

The woman said, "How strange?"

"What, for instance?" I repeated.

"All great artists love solitude, Hasan Bey."

"Like what, for instance?"

"Like yourself, for example...May I sit beside you?"

"Please, make yourself comfortable."

The woman sat beside me on an iron garden chair.

"Do you know, Hasan Bey, how much I have wanted to talk with you?"

"You mean you know me?"

"Oh, my dear sir, is there anyone who does not know your name? The whole country, the whole world knows you."

Something warm was spreading inside me and I relaxed. I tried to say something but I couldn't manage it.

The woman was talking.

"Believe me, because I have met you, this is the happiest night of my life."

I couldn't control my mouth which was stretching towards my cheeks. For whatever reason, my salivary glands started to work double time and a murmur emerged from between my drooling lips, "You are too kind."

"Not in the least! It is not kindness, I speak the truth. I have no right to praise a great artist like yourself but your true great value will be better understood with time."

I coughed in order to do something.

"You, due to the unfortunate backwardness of our country, are a writer whose worth is not properly understood."

Let's be honest about it, is there a writer who doesn't enjoy being complimented to his face? I was thoroughly relaxed and felt as though I were spreading out. I was on the point of melting with pleasure and sticking to where I sat.

"What a pity you were born in such a sterile country! There is no one who understands your genius."

My God, the woman thought the same about myself as I did.

"Where is the man who understands you? There's not a one!"

"If just one person could understand one, that happiness would be enough for a human being," I said.

"But is that the way things ought to be, Hasan Bey? Will you allow me to express my admiration for you?"

"You are too kind, dear lady. Would you be so kind as to tell me your name?"

"Süreyya, one of your admirers. Hasan Bey, you too, like all geniuses like to drink a lot, probably."

And so saying, she put into my hand a glass of that unknown drink on the table. Although I don't hold liquor well, in order to convince her of my genius, I said, "Yes, I drink a lot, till I go to sleep."

I emptied the glass in one gulp, my insides caught fire and flames spouted from my eyes.

"You are right. Without drinking, you couldn't ever write all those beautiful things."

"I start drinking as soon as I wake up in the morning and I keep on till I go to sleep."

"Who knows how little sleep you get, like all geniuses."

I can't keep going if I don't get eight to ten hours of uninterrupted sleep at night and I only sleep two hours after lunch, but I answered the woman's words, "It's not because I'm a genius but two or three hours sleep a night is enough for me. In fact, it's happened that I have gone for weeks and months without sleep."

Madam Süreyya called over the waiter who was passing by and, taking two glasses of that strong drink from the tray, said to the waiter, "Bring us a bottle of liquor and then stop here frequently. Don't leave the gentleman without anything to drink."

A little while later, the waiter brought a bottle full of the liquor.

Madam Süreyya said, raising her glass, "Cheers, maestro!"

White hot coals spread through my insides as I washed the drink down.

"Yes, plenty of people read your works, but I wonder how many of them grasp their profound meaning?"

"Ah...aaa, tonight you have re-opened old wounds."

I refilled from the bottle the glass I had emptied.

"Excuse me, maestro," she said, "but all great artists have their hobbies. What is your hobby?"

"Mine? My. . . my hobby?"

As a matter of fact, I have neither "hobbias" nor phobias. But I ought to have a hobby. At this point, the waiter brought another full bottle and took away the empty one.

"I raise crows in my house," I said. "My hobby is training crows."

"Very interesting...Cheers, maestro. May I ask you something else. I'm not making you uncomfortable, am I?"

"Oh no, on the contrary."

"Do you believe in luck? Do you have any superstitions? Well, all famous people do..."

"Of course, I have my superstitions too."

"For instance?"

"For instance...well...I don't know how to say this..."

I had opened up pretty thoroughly on account of the alcohol. The woman had pulled her chair up close to mine and pressed her arm against my own.

"With a woman..."

"I understand," she said. "Like all geniuses, you'll never grow old."

"Then," I said. "I believe in luck. Before I go out the door to the street, if I don't hop three steps, everything will go wrong that day. This is just for your ears alone. These are very private secrets."

After sighing deeply, she said, "How happy I am tonight. I thank you very much."

After tossing down a couple of drinks more, she said, "Excuse my curiosity, but I only ask out of the closeness and interest I feel. I know you understand my feelings. I want to know you better. My God, just to sit side by side with a genius!"

She had snuggled up to me pretty close. I had pulled back a little out of embarrassment but she had leaned on my shoulder.

"Please go ahead. Ask," I said.

"How do you write? What I mean is, do you have some peculiar habits? For example, when you are writing, do you soak your feet in hot water or do you sit in a steam bath, like other famous writers?"

I had downed another glass of liquor. On my empty stomach the liquor had completely gone to my head.

"No doubt about it," I said. "Before I start writing, I do

gymnastics. If I don't do gymnastics for exactly a half an hour, I can't get any inspiration."

"With or without instruments?"

"Both kinds of gymnastics. First, Swedish gymnastics, then I jump rope, then I lift weights. I toss a few Indian clubs. I do some chinups."

"I'm really impressed. Haven't you ever been in love, maestro?"

"OOOh, love?"

We both raised our glasses.

"I don't consider the seconds passed without love in my life to have been really lived."

Whereas the love in my whole life had consisted of that unfortunate declaration I just described that I made before rolling off the rock into the sea.

"Alas," I sighed, "I have never met with true love."

She caressed my chin with her hair. Then she took my hand and laid it to her eyes: she was crying!

"I too have never tasted true love," she said.

We took another drink. She stroked my face with hers. Just as a baby duckling learns to swim by instinct without a lesson, I understood by means of my male instincts that under such circumstances one should kiss a woman's lips. But for a man like myself in his sixties who had only kissed old ladies' hands in respect, kissing a woman's lips would have been ridiculous. My heart felt as though it were about to stop. I kissed Süreyya's hand in consternation. I had thought that when I kissed it, she would scold me and scream, "I'm not the kind of girl you think I am!" but she sighed, "Oooh, you've made me so happy!"

I too was happy.

I said, "The one who is really happy is me."

We pulled ourselves together when the waiter came. For the third time, he left the bottle on the table.

"Cheers."

After putting the glasses down, she said, "You are the greatest writer in the world: like Chekhov or de Maupassant."

Partly because of the liquor and partly because of the woman's continual flattery, I felt sure of myself for the first time in my life and so with the same momentum, I shouted, "I mean, who are Chekhov and de Maupassant?"

She said, with a docile voice, "You are as great as Balzac."

Now there were no longer any bounds to my bartering in greatness. I said, slamming down my fist on the iron table, "You mean you call Balzac a writer?"

"That's right, " she said. "You could only be compared, if at all, with Shakespeare."

By now I had gone off of the deep end and lost all sense of proportion because the woman had pretty thoroughly carried me away. As though saying "ptouhy", please excuse me, out of the corner of my mouth, I hissed, "Shakespeare! Shakespeare huh? What a shame. You don't understand me either."

And with the grief that this gave me, I drained a glass of that strong liquor.

"Oh, please, don't misunderstand me, " she said. "There is nobody in the world of literature who can be compared with you."

"Who was or is to come," I said.

"Yes," she said. "You are a God of literature."

I was amazed at how the woman could read what was going through my mind. For the first time in my life I was face to face with somebody who understood me.

"What I wanted to say," she said, "was that from time to time Shakespeare approaches you."

"Well, that could be," I said. "I can't help it if some foreigner of an Englishman who lived I don't know how many hundred years ago approaches me a little."

"You...you...you are greater than any of them. You are the greatest," she said.

Now she was using the familiar Turkish form of address to me.

"Naturally," I said.

"I love you, Hasan," she said.

I turned so giddy that I was about to fall right out of the chair I sat in, flat on the ground.

"You are my genius. One day you must receive the Nobel Prize."

"Do you think that the people who got the Nobel Prize have a different sort of tail from me? They are all of them monkeys," I said. "Naturally I'll get a Nobel. In fact I'll win it two or three times, you'll see."

"I believe in you, my beloved. I love you, Hasan."

"And I love you, Süreyya."

At that point, I began to use my head a little. Look here, I lived this long and not one woman ever encouraged me, so what was the matter with this one? Who told this woman that I was a fool? Didn't she think that I ever looked in a mirror once in my life? I will put up with anything but to be made a fool of, never!

Just at the instant when I was being gnawed by these doubts, Süreyya overturned her iron chair and fell onto the grass. She took me by the hand and pulled me to her side. I have no idea what to do in such a situation. That is to say, I do know, I've heard various things, as a male, from my friends, but because such a thing never happened to me before, I didn't know how to manage.

To escape from this difficult situation, I said, "What if somebody should see us?"

"Let them see! Let the whole world see, I don't care. Tonight I am the happiest woman in the world."

"My God, am I dreaming or have I died and have you taken me to Paradise?" I said to myself.

We lay, side by side, on the grass. She pillowed my head on her arm which she had stretched out under my neck.

To save myself from a very difficult situation in which I could not lie there like a log and in which I must do something but because, like a log, I could not do what seemed called for, I said, "Let's straighten ourselves out. Maybe the waiter will come."

"Let him come, let everybody come. Or maybe you're not happy?"

She was crying. It was then that I lost all my suspicions. What a stupid man I was. How could I doubt a woman who gave herself to me in such a way? So the saying, "love is blind" was true. Because she loved me, she couldn't see my actual shape or rather my shapelessness. Sureyya loved not my individual being but my artistic personality. Intellectual women were like that.

But some doubts still plagued me.

"Was what you said a little while ago true?" I said.

"What was that?"

"You know, that I was greater than Shakespeare?"

"Oh that? So you don't trust me?"

The empty glasses were refilled. Linking our arms, we drank from one another's hands. Sureyya's amorous acrobatics pleased me greatly.

Shouldn't I believe what she said? Wasn't the first person to believe in the Prophet his wife?

Then I had another misgiving. I hadn't seen the woman's face very clearly in the moonlight but it didn't seem ugly to me. Maybe she was crippled, hunchbacked, maimed. She must have something wrong with her. I could not conceive of a woman who could get a clean bill of health from a clinic, or even one that couldn't, falling for me or someone like me. I got up with the pretext of refilling the bottle. She got up too. My purpose was to see her in the moonlight and I did: she was a wonder, every line and feature were wonderful.

We went back into the darkness, me with the refilled bottle in my hand. I sat on the chair so we wouldn't have to lie on the grass anymore and she sat on a chair as well. We kept on drinking.

"Who knows how many woman you have had in your life?" she said.

When she said this, I was holding my glass to my lips. I put the glass on the table, after having sneezed out the liquor that had got up my nose.

After I had pulled myself together, I said, "I don't . . . all that much."

"Don't try to deny it. You have them . . . you have them."

"I do certainly but I don't attach importance to women. I don't pay attention to a one."

"I know their type. Even if you don't pay them any attention, they pester you to death."

"Yes, to tell the truth, they drive me crazy."

"Perhaps you think I'm one of those women?"

"You are the first woman ever to understand me."

"They run after you for your fame but I love you because you are Hasan."

While our conversation had been going on so sweetly up to this point, suddenly she insisted, "Tell me all about the women in your life!"

Even though I said, "Sweetheart, how can I do that? A man doesn't do that sort of thing. You know I couldn't do that," I made no impression on her.

Tossing down another glass of liquor, I asked her, "Are you talking about my past affairs?"

"No, the ones you have now."

"There's a blond."

"Is she married?"

"The married one is somebody else. Then there is a widow and two brunettes."

"Who else?"

"There's an auburn-haired one but don't tell anybody."

"What's her name?"

"Now that I can't tell you."

"So that's the way it is?" she said. "You are hiding things from me."

"My dearest, would I hide anything from you at all? But..."

"As if I didn't know her name. It's Shukran!"

"No, Shukran is somebody else. This one is thinner."

"Is that all there is?"

"There are others but I can't even remember their names."

She wasn't content with this and she insisted that I tell her about my affairs with all these women, no matter what. I made up a yarn for each one.

Sureyya was crying. She laid her head on my chest and she said, shaken by sobs, "I'm jealous. I am a jealous woman, Hasan. Hasan, be mine alone!"

"From this moment forth, I am yours, Süreyya, I belong to you."

I don't understand why I didn't ask her about the affairs she had had and the men in her life but she told me all by herself. She had been married four times but she hadn't been happy in any of the marriages and had led a sad existence. She had never found a man who understood her soul whereas her broken heart had thirsted after happiness.

Because what she told me touched me so much, I couldn't control myself and I burst into tears.

"Just one man has come into my life who can understand my soul and that is you, Hasan," she said.

The tears from our pressed-together faces mingled and we wept to our hearts' content.

The last train home was at one-thirty. I looked at my watch: it was one o'clock. The station was far away. It would take a half hour to get there. I got up.

"You're leaving?"

"I can't stay, the last train..."

Just then, a male voice resounded through the garden, "Süreyya, Süreyya..."

"My uncle is calling me. My family is leaving probably."

"Where do you live?"

"In Yeshilkoy."

"How will you get all the way to Yeshilkoy after midnight?"

"In my uncle's car. My aunt and the children are with us.

I was just about to tell her that I couldn't live without her, when she said, "I can't live without you any longer, Hasan. Can I trust you?"

"Trust me!" I said.

"Swear it!"

"On my honor."

"Now I believe you."

"Now *you* swear."

"If I lie, may I kiss your corpse."

The uncle was still shouting "Süreyya" in the garden. We couldn't part from one another.

She said, "If I lose you, I'll kill myself."

"I too..."

"Let's meet tomorrow."

"Where?"

"At Florya. We can go to the beach."

"What time?"

"Be at the beach at nine o'clock, at the gate to Paradise Beach."

"No, no, I don't want to wait for you at beach gates. I'll be on the beach at nine o'clock and you can find me, only don't keep me waiting."

We embraced. Whenever I cry, my nose runs. Although I sniffed as hard as I could, still my nose wet Süreyya's beautiful cheeks when I kissed her.

"Till we meet again, my beloved."

"Good-bye, Hasan."

Süreyya walked towards the brightly lighted mansion. I started towards the station. I hadn't even seen the Ex-Minister. Just then I couldn't have cared less about ministers, old or new.

The road from the hill where the mansion was to the station passed through open country. I know very well that I set out on that road but then I found myself on a slope, in an untilled field in the middle of thickets and briar bushes. I was lost. I was so happy that not only could I have gone over hill and dale but if I had flapped my arms, I could have flown. I was drunk with love. Just with love? I was rolling drunk with love, reeling drunk with liquor and tight with the beauty of the starry night.

In my pleasure, I started to murmur a song. For a while I clawed my way up the hillsides and down the slopes, singing my song. After a while, I realized that what I was murmuring was not a song but the "Ten Year Anniversary of the Republic March" because I don't know any classical Turkish song or folk ballad. You know how the March starts, "We set forth in proud success..." To tell the truth, I hadn't left Süreyya very proudly or successfully. I had set out very clumsily. I decided that it wasn't right to sing the March. I started repeating, "The first woman to ever understand me..." I repeated "The first woman to ever understand me..." over and over again as a song. Although I don't know music, I had composed this song all by myself and every time I sang it, the notes were different, at times it was an Arab love song, at times an Italian aria, at times it was a Turkish folk song or a march or even a hymn. To be more exact, that's how I thought it was.

As I was going along, staggering and wobbling through the stones and thickets, falling down and getting up, bawling, "The first woman to ever understand me" at the top of my voice, the ground beneath my feet gave way and I found my seventy-nine kilo body in a hole. I hit hard places as I rolled down and ended up sitting on a wet surface. Since people don't sit on their heads, I can't call what I did "sit" because what hit the bottom was my head and my feet were in the air. After I had pulled myself together, I explored where I was, feeling with my hands but I couldn't figure it out. It could have been a dry well, the dried-up bed of a stream, the pit for a building, a newly dug foundation for a house or a septic tank for a summer house. Whatever sort of place it was, I didn't want to destroy the happy, pleasant mood I was in. After I had found a depression to rest my back against and stretched my feet out, I began to sing the love song whose scale, tempo and notes changed every time I sung it,

"The firrrssst wooman to eever understaaand me!"

I was so happy that I could have sung love songs in that pit till the break of day but all of a sudden when I remembered that I was to meet Süreyya at Florya at nine o'clock, I sprang up. I looked at the illuminated dial of my watch: it was two o'clock. I had missed the last train. It would be three o'clock when I got home, if I could find a taxi. To get to Florya by nine, I would have to leave the house at the latest at six o'clock. If I were to oversleep, I wouldn't get to Florya by nine and then I would be disgraced.

I got up and jumped up. I shouted again and again and jumped as though this would get me out of the hole. To strengthen my morale, I jumped again, bawling and yelling like Tarzan but whatever I might do, I couldn't get out of the hole. All this struggling about didn't accomplish anything except tear my clothes and leave my hands and face bloodied. If I had continued to struggle, I would have torn my clothes to shreds and left my body...excuse the expression...in a state of "strip tease". With one last effort, I finally rolled onto the road, hitting the rocks as I did so. It seemed that I had not been in a pit but at the foot of an outcropping of rocks with a very steep slope on one side, a little to one side of the road. It was then that I knew that I was drunk. I must have drunk too much of that strong liquor because I had got into a state where I couldn't distinguish the road from the hillside.

All at once, I thought of the book, the important book I had borrowed from my friend's library to read for a couple of days. I had left the book in the place where I had made love to Süreyya, on top of the table. Whatever the liquor was that I had drank, I had lost my senses. That is, I'm not against liquor. Two or three times in my life I have drunk a glass of raki to a friend's health in order not to be a spoilsport but the thing I drank that night was worse than raki.

The book was very valuable and rare. Now whatever I did, if I went back to pick up the book, I would be late for everything.

I wouldn't be at Florya at nine o'clock. I would telephone my friend the Ex-Minister early in the morning and ask him to take good care of my book. I hurried on towards the station. Every so often I would stagger and fall but when I got up again, I would decide the direction I had to go and walk straight on towards the station. Since I had missed the last train, I would get in a taxi at the station, if I could find one.

Finally, I saw the station lights but these didn't look like the dim lights you're accustomed to see in stations. The entire station was bathed in lights of every color, shining brightly. Even if that night had been a national holiday, the station wouldn't have been lit up like that!

As I got closer and closer, I saw that this was not the place I was familiar with but was a different, charming station. There were cars in a row in front of the door. Not a one was a taxi, they were all private cars.

Some of the drivers had gathered around one of the cars and were kidding around.

Approaching them, I said, "Please excuse me, but what station is this?"

What should a ruffian driver say to me but "Edirne station"?

"It can't be Edirne! I'm on the Anatolian side, I haven't crossed the sea to get to Edirne. Don't make fun of me. Tell the truth! Where is this?"

Another driver, who from his speech had obviously been well brought up, said, "Hey, look it, don't kid the old gent. Why are you fooling the guy, damn it?"

Turning to me, he said, "This is Adapazar station, old timer."

"My God!"

"What surprised you so much?"

"A little while ago, I left a house hereabouts. I got to Adapazar in a hurry. Good for me, I must have walked fast, considering how many times I fell down on the road."

The driver asked me, "The house you said you left, what province was it in? Was it in Malatya or in Diyarbakir?"

"No, that's ridiculous. It was in Istanbul, for pity's sake. Excuse me but it's almost morning. Why is this Adapazar station all lit up?"

"Haven't you heard? It was in all the papers. They installed broken glass in the station windows and that's what the festivities are about. Don't you hear all the laughing? They are having a banquet."

The rude fellows were making fun of me. I walked to the station. The bursts of laughter were truly getting louder. What should I see when I looked in the window? It was nothing other than the house of my friend the Ex-Minister that I had just left! I had come back to the house I had just left, soaked in a sweat after having fallen all over the road and changed my direction again and again, thinking that I was heading towards the station.

But what was this insane, choking laughter of the people inside all about? Nobody was left in the garden or on the terrace. They had all gone into the reception room. Going onto the terrace, I peeked in the window. My beloved Süreyya was telling something and the others were laughing in bursts of merriment. Some were laughing as though they would choke to death, others were rolling on the floor and kicking their legs in the air. Some were weeping from laughter.

A fat woman shrieked, "Oh, please, Süreyya, hush, hush now. I swear, you're going to make me mess myself. Hush, girl."

From the place where I stood behind the shutter, the people inside couldn't see me. But I could hear Süreyya.

"I never saw such a stupid fellow in all my life. Oh what a dummy! 'You are a misunderstood genius', I said. 'I too am a misunderstood, unfortunate woman, Hasan Bey," I said. I got him to drink and drink. I kept acting as though I was drinking and poured it out on the ground. When he got high, the fellow got so silly. Before he sat down to write, he said he did gymnastics for a half an hour to get his inspiration. He actually said, 'Who is Balzac compared to me'!"

Whatever we had said to one another in the utmost confidence, she retold, exaggerating as she went and adding on a thousand things to make her hearers scream with laughter.

My friend the Ex-Minister said, wiping the tears of mirth

from his eyes, "I know. He's the king of fools. I can just see him now."

A woman asked, "Did he declare his love on bended knee?"

Süreyya said, "Of course, and the big old fellow sobbed and cried too, like he was howling."

The people who crowded the reception room were rocked by another cyclone of laughter.

Slowly, I withdrew from the window. I had sobered up pretty thoroughly by now and I set out on my road. There was no taxi at the station. I couldn't find any way to get home. I thought over why Süreyya would do something like that as I was waiting for morning on a bench in the station waiting room. At last I understood the reason why. They had seen us together and had gossiped about it. The poor woman had had to tell those lies to save her reputation from the gossips because otherwise Süreyya was not the woman to betray the oath she had sworn to remain faithful to our love.

The next morning, I took the first train to Haydarpaşa and went on from there by ferry to the Bridge. First I bought a pair of swimming trunks and then I went by train to Florya. I went to the beach that Süreyya had told me to. Nine o'clock, ten o'clock, twelve o'clock, two o'clock. There wasn't a place I didn't look on the beach. Who knew what awful disaster had overtaken the poor girl to keep her from coming to the beach, otherwise she would have certainly come.

I waited till seven in the evening without losing a bit of hope. I would have waited longer but a woman in a bikini who was lying facedown on the sand said to me, grinning, "Mister, this is probably your first trip to the beach."

"Yes," I said. "This is my first trip, today. But how did you know?"

"Your skin is so white. You don't have any tan but your back is very burned. You won't sleep tonight from the soreness. If you like I can rub some of this cream on your back. It will help the sunburn."

Without waiting for my answer, she came and sat down

beside me and started to daub on my back the liquid that she poured out of the bottle into her palm. A warm, soft breeze caressed the places that she passed her hand over.

I murmured to myself, "The first woman ever to understand me!"

The woman said, "What was that?"

"Nothing", I said.

The woman said, "Thirty liras," and she laughed and I saw the gold plated teeth between her thick lips.

I laughed too.

"Shall we go in a booth?" she said.

"Who does that fellow Balzac think he is?" I said.

"Who is that? Is he somebody who's giving you a hard time?"

"I'll get Nobel yet," I said.

"Oh, I get it," she said. "This Nobel your talking about is some broad you're fighting over with this guy. Right? I really feel for you. Come on, forget Nobel. Come on, get up!"

"Let's lie right here on the sand. It's better that way," I said.

"Alright, give me twenty," she said.

"I'll pay you thirty but stay here," I said.

I laid my head on the woman's thigh. Not exactly like that, how could I lay my head there? The woman grabbed me by the nape of the neck as though she were practicing Turkish wrestling and laid my head on her thigh.

"Nobel should shine your shoes," she said.

"The first woman ever to understand me," I said.

"Who?" she asked.

"You!" I said.

We Resemble You

("Biz Size Benzeriz" from *Rifat Bey Neden Kaşınıyor,*
1965)

On the eve of the announcement of the new mayor's election,
a number of city officials, department chiefs, typists and male
and female bureaucrats who had come in from other offices
had gathered in a large room in the city hall of a large town
and were all talking together with great joy.

"Oh, how happy I was, if you only knew. I can't tell you,
really."

"Anybody would be happy. I cried from happiness, I promise
you."

"And how do you think I felt? I couldn't sleep all night for
being so happy."

"Ever since we learned that Bekir Bey had been elected, we
have had a continual party in our house. My granny, old a lady
as she is, jumped up and skipped around snapping her fingers,
can you imagine?"

"I swear before God, folks, Allah knows what is inside me
anyway so why should I hide it from you? I have been praying
continually for Bekir Bey to be elected."

"And me? I even promised a candle to Elekchi Dede, the holy dervish. We lit the candles last night."

"I don't want to brag but I got at least five hundred people to vote for Bekir Bey."

"I don't care if I do say so. He's a really good man."

"Come on, 'good' isn't the word for him. He's a fatherly person. He's the father of the poor and needy."

"I know, I know him very well. His aunt was a tenant in the house next door to my mother's house in Salmayashak. In fact, once it was a holiday and they came to kiss her hand."

"That's right. He's very respectful towards older people."

"Well, sir, whatever you may say, he is a well brought up person. People with that old fashioned training are special."

"I, my humble self, know him well, sir. Years ago he used to be a member of the city council, but what a member! So collected, so reflected, so respected, so well selected, so con..."

"I don't care what any of you say, none of you know him as well as I do. We're relatives. My brother-in-law is the same as Bekir Bey's cousin. The husband of the sister-in-law of the first husband of my brother-in-law's mother-in-law is the brother of Bekir Bey's stepmother. That makes us cousins, because my uncle..."

"Forget about your uncle. You can't know him like I do. Friendship counts more than being relations. He's my big brother's best friend. They always sit side by side at every ball game in Mithat Pasha Stadium. In fact, once I said to my brother..."

"Look, don't tell us about your brother. I worked in his office. Does your brother know him like I do?"

"He doesn't know him like you do but still he knows him."

"He's amazingly polite, for one thing."

"He is."

"Amazingly."

"He's amazingly unassuming."

"Then, you know, he's very something or other."

"Naturally."

"We're classmates. I know him very well. He was a very

clever boy. You could see that, even back then. All the teachers used to say, 'Look, this child is going to be mayor when he grows up.' "

"And sir, the man is just made to be mayor."

"He answered all his greeting cards. Look at the cards in my wallet. 'Wishing you an equally happy holiday. Warmest best wishes'."

"He's very charitable."

"Veeery."

"I saw this with my own eyes. It was in a bus, I had a package in my hand. In fact, I will never forget this, it was a package of pistachio nut sweets I had bought at Hajibekir's. He got up right away and said, 'Please sit down madam', and gave me his place but I know he didn't have any bad designs on me."

"No, he didn't."

"But if he had wanted to..."

"If he had wanted to, that would have been different."

"Oh, now look! Why wouldn't he? Or am I not..."

"He's an upright man."

"He's a moral family man, *efendim*. He doesn't look at anyone's wife or daughter."

"I worked in his office and I know. If he wanted to, hohoho, all the good looking women and girls around. But believe me, he doesn't even glance at a one of them."

"I wonder why. Is he a whatyoucallit?"

"What do you mean? He has three children and he's very religious."

"That's for certain. How many times I've seen him at the Eyub Sultan Shrine on Fridays as I was passing by."

"Bravoo."

"If you will allow me, I will tell you an incident. One morning, I don't know how it happened but I was a little late in getting to the office. If we didn't run into one another in the doorway? Do you know what he said to me? 'Your watch is probably three minutes late,' he said. Hahaha."

"You don't say so! What a witty man."

"He's very clever."

"There's a witticism in everything he says, sir, whatever you may say. Just think about those words, 'Your watch is three minutes late, probably.' "

"I am just crazy over the way he smokes his cigarettes. I never miss a movie and I've seen loads of actors smoking cigarettes but nobody smokes like he does."

"Yeees, he smokes his cigarettes well."

"Sir, you can tell a man from the way he handles his raki. My humble self, I saw Bekir Bey..."

"Did you drink together?"

"No, I don't like to tell lies. They were drinking in a restaurant in Beyoglu at the table next to mine. My humble self, I also saw him while I was walking down the street. They were doing some serious drinking."

"*Efendim*, the man has breeding. Breeding is something special. He's very well bred."

"His mother was Hayrünnisa Hanimefendi, one of the most pious of Muslim women and..."

"May Allah grant her peace. May Allah grant Bekir Bey long years of life."

"His father was an important man as well."

"Wasn't he the Kadi of the Hijaz?"

"Yes, probably."

"Is it true that his grandfather won the battle of Kosova?"

"That's right and it wasn't just Kosova. It was Mohac as well."

"They say that he was at The Dardenelles."

"Yes, he was. When the boat he was traveling on ran aground, he stayed at Gallipoli for three days."

"Good heavens!"

"He received a head wound. He fell down the stairs of the hotel he was staying at."

"You don't say."

"What a shame."

"Isn't that fantastic?"

"*Efendim*, the most amazing thing about him is that if you locked him up in the treasury, he wouldn't steal ten *paras*."

"Isn't that amazing? Really!"

"He himself doesn't steal but how many times he has let pickpockets rob him!"

"Bravo, what an honest man."

"In fact..."

"Now everything is going to get straightened out, you'll see."

"The people were lucky that they have got a man like that as a mayor."

"This world doesn't hang upon the ox's horn for such people..."

"It sits on its shoulder!"

A few days after the return of the election results, the election committee, having found that the objections made to it were factual, nullified the votes that Bekir Bey had received. It was announced that someone else had been elected mayor and the news was published in the papers. In the same big room of the city hall of the big town, the same people, a few absent and few others present, were talking together in great joy.

"Oh, how happy I was, how happy, if you only knew. I can't tell you, I assure you."

"Wouldn't anybody be happy? Why, the fellow was almost here on top of us. We had a lucky escape."

"When I heard he had been elected, something happened to me. I lost my appetite."

"I cried. What if he had come here?"

"We would really have had it."

"Allah had mercy on us."

"We must still have good deeds we have to perform."

"When they said that Bekir Bey had been elected, I couldn't sleep all night, I was so sad."

"I tell you, people, God knows this so why should I hide it

from you, I prayed all the time that Bekir Bey wouldn't be elected."

"All my neighbors were going to vote for him but I persuaded at least five hundred not to."

"Good for you."

"If that fellow had been elected mayor, I swear before God, I wouldn't have stayed here another minute. I would have resigned right away."

"Who would have stayed on?"

"Come on, you can't resign."

"That's true but I would have requested a transfer to somewhere else."

"You don't know him, what he's like."

"Who? Me? I don't know him? Me, is it? My dear, I don't think anybody knows him as well as I do. His aunt was a servant in my mother's house in Salmayashak. One time he came and didn't even speak to his aunt or his mother. How do you like that?"

"That's true. He's very conceited."

"He has a swell head."

"He's an upstart. He looks down on everybody."

"*Efendim*, what can you expect? He was badly brought up. Anyway, he is a social climber."

"I even lit a candle to Elekchi Dede, the saint, and prayed that anybody be elected as long as it was not this fellow. Allah heard my prayer and we went to Elekchi Dede last night and lighted more candles."

"May God hear your prayers."

"He's an upstart, *beyim*, an upstart. Say what you will, the fellow is a come-lately upstart and that's that. I know him and I can say it: the fellow has no breeding, so put that in your pipe and smoke it."

"I know him well. Years ago he was a city council member and there wasn't anything he didn't do wrong. He was so imperious, so salacious, so vicious, so ambitious, so seditious, so..."

"I don't care what you say, you don't know him as well as I do. Unfortunately they say that he is the neighbor of a distant, oooh, a very distant relative of ours, but I don't know. None of the family have anything to do with those relatives. They don't even speak to them."

"Never mind that. You can't know any better than I do. I know him from school days. He was lazy, good-for-nothing, a clown, a vagabond of a boy. In fact, our teachers used to show him to us and say, 'If this thing here ever amounts to anything, all the mangy dogs in the street will turn into important people.' Just think of that!"

"None of you know what I do about him. Oh, no, I don't know him but my big brother saw him a couple of times in Mithat Pasha Stadium. He used to yell 'dummmmy' at the referee. Yes, 'dummy'."

"Was 'dummy ' all he said?"

"Please excuse me but he shouted 'youknowwhat' too."

"Oh, no! That's a shame."

"Look, folks, we've had a narrow escape."

"And how! We can congratulate ourselves this far."

"Each and everyone and the whole country, the country..."

"I can't tell you how you know he is."

"He's so self-centered. He'd youknowwhat for three piasters."

"Now, I didn't want to tell this but now I have to. I don't know how many times, I'm ashamed to say this, he made passes at me. Ayten even saw it. If Ayten was here she could tell you. Of course I didn't pay him any attention."

"The lowdown fellow!"

"My dear, if he was the last man left in this world and I turned and looked down my nose at him, don't call me a human being."

"Who would look at the ugly rascal?"

"He has no taste. He even chases servants."

"*Efendim*, he's a compulsive womanizer."

"How do you know?"

"That's what they say. You know that where there's smoke, there's fire."

"I don't know about the other stuff, *beyim*, but if a man is a phony, he's no good. He drinks raki in the daytime during Ramazan and then visits Eyub Sultan Shrine acting as if he were fasting just to show off."

"May Allah..."

"Naturally..."

"If you will allow me I will relate a recollection. One day he came to the office at eleven o'clock. I couldn't take it. 'Beyefendi, Beyefendi,' I said, ' 'Tis morn in Scutari.' Where were you so late that you let your lantern go out?' I said."

"Good for you."

"He didn't even let out a peep. He turned red as a beet."

"He worked in my office years ago. I know him very well but I don't even speak to him."

"What about the way he smokes like a chimney? And that cigarette that hangs from his lip. Ugh, how disgusting!"

"Men show their true natures when they drink raki, *beyim*."

"Did you used to drink together?"

"Heavens, no. I saw him when he used to drink with other people. He's insolent, rude, aggressive. He drinks and drinks and then, in the end, excuse me, he throws up and won't leave unless you beat him."

"He drinks himself under the table."

"He does."

"He's impotent."

"I, my poor self, don't know, but so they say."

"Efendim, there is nothing as important as family. Degeneracy really comes from the family, because..."

"They say, 'like breeds like'."

"Is it true that his grandfather had whatyoucallit?"

"Everybody knows that. In fact, it says on his identity card," (whisper, whisper, whisper, in his ear.)

"Allah, Allah!"

"Yeees."

"Weren't we lucky?"

"Do you know who was elected mayor in his place?"

"They say it's Hayri Bey."

"Oh, wonderful, great. He's a fine man."

"Marvelous. In fact, I, my humble self..."

The Made-To-Order Funeral Oration

("Ismarlama Cenaze Söylevi" from *Rifat Bey Neden Kaşınıyor?*, 1965)

Once upon a time, I had just gotten out of jail where they had stuck me I-don't-know-how-many times. I had no work, money or friends. An acquaintance who knew my situation said, "Look here, it's really a shame."

"You're right," I said.

"So why are you doing it this way?"

"What am I supposed to do?"

"Come on and let me introduce you to somebody who needs someone like yourself."

He took me to see a man. He was a shoemaker but he was making good money. He sold shoes wholesale to the big stores and mostly made the high heeled women's footwear that was in style in those days.

Those were the days when democracy had just been imported into Turkey and everybody was crazy to be elected a representative to the National Assembly. Nobody was listening to anybody else and everybody was talking at once. Everybody was going to rescue and rebuild Turkey.

It was election time. This shoemaker had registered as an

independent candidate and had completed all the formalities, only he didn't have a speech to pronounce to the people in the public squares. If he only could find a couple of speeches and memorize them, he would have the job of deputy to the Assembly and it would be all his, to use as his heart's desired.

"There are so many thousand workers in this country," he would say. "All the workers know me," he would say. "I will protect the workers' rights," he would say. "If that many workers who know me, give me that many votes, it will do the job," he would say.

It was obvious that he had some *veeery* important ideas that would develop Turkey, presto. However "due to his lack of formal education," he couldn't write them down. It turned out that I was supposed to be the "very effective election speech" ghostwriter who would enable him to speak to the people from the election platform.

I wrote the speech. It went something like this, as I remember:

"Oh brother laborers, who have nought to lose but your torn stockings! You can't even wear the cloth you weave. You can't put on the shoes you make. You can't live in the houses you build. They dress up and you stay barefooted and ragged. You have worked for the benefit of others long enough! You have made everything there is but you yourselves are not allowed the benefits of it. The sweat of your brows and the light of your eyes is turned into office buildings and apartment houses for the ones who exploit you. Enough of this oppression, enough of this torture..."

You couldn't say things like that in those days. (Nowadays, you know, you can.) The man liked the speech very much. The friend who had introduced us gave me ten liras he got from him. I later found out that he had gotten twenty liras, kept ten liras as his cut and given me the ten, God bless him. They paid between two and a half and five liras in those days for the finest short stories. I wished there were a market for it so that I could write twenty speeches like that a day.

He started to learn his speech as independent candidate by heart but the man didn't have a brain in his head. He would confuse "you" with "they". For instance, instead of saying, "They take their ease in apartment houses like palaces while you shiver with cold in huts with leaky roofs", he would say "You take your ease in apartment houses like palaces while they shiver with cold in huts with leaky roofs."

I just barely got the man to memorize it. The speech must have been the "very effective" thing he had wanted because at the exact beginning of the speech, the police dragged the man off of the platform and hauled him to the Directorate of Security.

They grilled him, asking him, "Who wrote this?"

Because he sensed that he would be sorry he had ever been born if he turned me in, he said, "I had one of the scribes in the court of Yenicami Mosque write it, but who he was, I don't know."

He wasn't able to save his skin that easily but after he had shown them that he was a "solid and self-respecting citizen" by proving that he had shops and stores and was the owner of a business and a workshop and had money in the bank, he escaped from the clutches of the police.

When he saw that the speech was roundly applauded, he truly got the idea of becoming a representative into his head and had me write him a couple of other speeches.

That is how we became even better acquainted. Someone else was elected but even though my man wasn't elected, it was due one hundred per cent to bad luck because he wasn't any the less able than the ones that were actually elected.

Whenever he needed something written or when he didn't know what to do, he would come to me.

Finally, it was time for his daughter to get married. He was going to have to make a speech at her wedding. The groom was from a prominent family and so as not to appear inferior to them and to show that he was an intelligent man, he wanted to give a solid speech. I wrote a speech wishing the newlyweds happiness. He left a fifty lira bill on the table as though he were leaving the fee for a visit to the doctor. I was well off at that time and one of my stories would bring a hundred liras. I didn't take his money.

"Please," he said, "every effort has to be rewarded. If you won't accept my money, I won't come to you any more for this kind of work."

"Come whenever you want and I'll write whatever you want."

Later, according to what I was told, the wedding speech was quite amusing. He frequently forgot what he had tried to memorize and would take the paper with the speech on it out of his pocket and read a few lines. However, in the same pocket where he had put the paper with speech on it, was the order invoice for how many women's shoes he was supposed to send to which stores.

"My beloved children! As you walk down the hard road of life joyful and happy, hand in hand..."

He had forgotten the rest! He pulled the invoice paper out of his pocket, thinking it was the speech paper. Because he read syllable by syllable and it was hard for him to unravel the letters, he himself didn't understand what he was reading.

"My beloved children! As you walk down the hard road of life, joyful and happy, hand in hand, twenty pairs of high heels to Christaki's on the Beach. Thirty pairs of fancy styles to the Three Star Shoe Store..."

So the wedding was very amusing.

One day he came back to my house.

"Look," he said, "my son is studying in Germany to be an engineer. He's been in Germany for four years. Now he put it in his head that he can't stand the homesickness and he's going to come on home. It's a shame. Please, write him a stirring poem so that he will read it and stay where he is."

From what I got from his son's letter, even if he stayed there not four or five but four or five thousand years, not only would he not be an engineer but he wouldn't even make a house painter. The son was more of a rapscallion than the father. His intention was just to squeeze some more money out of his father.

The boy's name was Hurshit. I wrote a verse and I still remember it:

> *The chick that hatches from his shell seeks not the*
> *shell but feed to eat,*
> *The horse, if Arab steed he be, longs for the finest*
> *shoing for his feet.*
> *This world to which we've come to work and strive*
> *is all a foreign shore,*
> *He who will labor hard must tire himself but in the*
> *end his wants placate.*

> *Do not despair because on foreign strand thou art.*
> *The stranger who knowledge gains stays not for-*
> *ever there but timely winds him home,*
> *Hurshit my son, who is there who from hearth and*
> *home has never strayed?*
> *Endure my child, who labors hard one day will*
> *find both fame and name.*

Once more he offered me money and I refused.

"But I'll be ashamed to come back any more," he said.

"We are old friends. You gave me work when I was in dire straights. Come anytime, I'll be glad to see you," I said.

I didn't see him for years but recently he came to see me again.

"My father-in-law has passed away," he said.

"My condolences," I said.

"The funeral is going to be tomorrow at such and such a mosque," he said.

"Very good," I said.

Now that I had so much work to do, I certainly didn't have time to go to his father-in-law's funeral and why should I anyway?

When he saw that I was unconcerned he said, "I have a request to make of you again."

"Please go on, what is it?"

"A speech to be said at the grave side..."

"I have more than I can handle right now but you are an old friend."

"Oh, no," he said. "I can't read it, don't you see?"

"Somebody else can read it."

"You can read it. Please, don't refuse me this favor."

"What? You want me to speak at your father-in-law's funeral? I can't do that. For one thing, I didn't know him and then why should I?"

He begged and pleaded.

"These are not the days when you used to write election speeches for me. You are a famous person. Everybody knows you. It would be something special if you would speak at my father-in-law's grave. Didn't you say, 'We're old friends'?"

I understood what he was after. Even in a business like this he had an underhanded motive. He was going to show off to his circle of friends and say that so and so had spoken at his father-in-law's funeral.

I am too much of a softy to just cut him off and tell him that I wouldn't do such a thing and get rid of the man. I understood that there was no escape from his wheedling. Otherwise he would say behind my back, "When he didn't have two coins to rub together he wrote election speeches for me at ten liras apiece and now that he thinks he's somebody, he's got a swell head."

"Very well," I said. "What were your father-in-law's traits? What did he do for a living?"

"You shouldn't speak ill of the dead but, God have mercy on his soul, he was a scoundrelly fellow."

"You can't say that at the graveside. Tell me something nice about him."

"Well, there wasn't anything good about the dirty rascal."

"Tell me about his life."

"Once upon a time he was a volunteer fireman, one of our old time gangs of firemen. A ruffian...He was a draft dodger. They arrested him and put him in the army when he was forty years old."

"It took him exactly ten years to finish his military service because he kept running off. He went to prison a couple of times because of fights, murders, police raids. That was the kind of scoundrel he was. Now that he's dead, there's one less dirty swine in the country."

"What do you expect me to say at the grave of a man like that?"

"You'll think of something to say. You'll make something up. Nobody but you can do it. Don't disappoint me."

The next day I went to the mosque where the funeral service was to take place after the noon prayers.

There were five other funerals. A good number of wreathes had arrived. Whatever happened took place when they were putting the deceased into the hearses. It was so crowded that I couldn't catch sight of anybody I knew and, pushing and shoving, I climbed into a taxi with some other people. There was a row of taxis there, taxis that the mourners had rented. I got into the wrong one, into one of the taxis that another mourner had rented.

We went to the graveyard. The coffins were being put in the ground and to one side the imams, the reciters and the paid mourners were reciting the Koran. I had gone by mistake to the funeral of a very pious, very philanthropic and very rich woman who had made the Pilgrimage to Mecca two times.

I looked all around for my friends but they were nowhere to be seen. I said to myself that I couldn't see them for the crowd in any case and who knows where they were huddled, crying crocodile tears. It never entered my mind that I had gone to the wrong grave.

The coffin was put in the ground, the grave was filled up but when it came time to lay the wreaths on the top of the grave, there was a mixup. The wreaths from different funerals got exchanged. The mourners started to sort out the wreaths from the different funerals. The wreath from the Chamber of Industry went that way and the wreath from the Association of Tradesmen went the other. When this error of wreaths was settled, thinking it was now my turn, I went to the head of the grave mound and began speaking:

"The Deceased was an important figure in the history of sports in our country."

I heard a few murmurs but I thought that the murmurs were expressions of grief.

"The Deceased played an immortal role in the history of athletics in our country. As you know, the volunteer firemen's gangs are considered to be the first athletic clubs in our country and the Deceased performed great services to our volunteer firemen."

"The Deceased was a great patriot, having actually done military service for ten years and completed that patriotic duty with honor."

The murmurs increased. I heard things like "Shut him up," "Who is this guy anyway?" "Where did he come from?" but I thought that these were the effects of sorrow.

"The Deceased suffered all the oppression of the antidemocratic era through long years of incarceration in the prisons and..."

The muttering had reached a high level and the crowd marched towards me and surrounded me. They probably thought I was having fun with them and were preparing to give me a sound hiding when my friend came running like the wind and broke through the crowd.

"Did our wreaths get mixed up with yours?" he cried.

When he saw me there, he said, "Where have you been? I have been looking for you since morning."

In fact, his father-in-law's wreaths had gotten mixed up with those that were where I was. There were the wreaths that two banks had sent and three wreaths from individuals as well.

He put three of the wreaths on his back and I took two of them and we took them to the grave of his father-in-law but the crowd had broken up. Naturally I didn't give a speech beside the grave. We put the wreaths down, my friend paid off the Koran reciters and the professional mourners. Together we climbed into a car and went home.

On the way he said, "What a shame! You didn't get to speak at the grave."

"What can we do? Even the wreaths and the mourners got mixed up."

"May I ask you something?" he said.

"Please go ahead," I said.

"Since you have gone to the trouble to write that thing, would you see that it was printed in a paper so that it won't be lost?" he said.

To get rid of him, I said, "Of course, I'll have it published somewhere."

When he was getting out of the car and taking his leave, he said, "Can I say something? You gave your speech in the right place after all. My father-in-law, he was buried in the grave that you spoke over, you know, and that old lady was buried in our grave. When they were lowering the coffin I caught on but why start a lot of trouble, brother? Should I start a big fuss over 'That body is yours and this body is mine'? Just look at the wreaths. What is underneath the ground isn't important."

Don't You Have Any Donkeys In Your Country

("Sizin Memlekette Eşek yok mu?"
from *Rıfat Bey Neden Kaşınıyor?*, 1965)

He came in shaking his head from side to side, holding his hand to his face as though he had the toothache. He kept alternately slapping his hand to his face and saying, "Damn it, I've been disgraced. I've been disgraced."

Notwithstanding, he was a very well bred man. I was quite surprised that he would start flagellating himself, saying, "Damn it, I've been disgraced", the minute he walked in the door, before he even greeted me.

"Please come in," I said. "Make yourself at home, please sit down."

"I'm disgraced. I'm disgraced."

"How are you?"

"How do you think I am? Is there anything else I can be? I'm disgraced, that's all there is to it, damn it all."

I thought he had suffered a disaster, maybe a misfortune concerning his family.

"I feel like crawling into a hole. I'm not worth two paras, two paras."

"Why? What happened to you?"

143

"I don't know what more could happen. They sold a man a broken down, mangy donkey for two thousand five hundred liras."

I drew back and peered into his face. Was he crazy perhaps?

Frankly, I was scared. I said, as an excuse for calling my wife, "Would you like a coffee?"

"Forget the coffee," he said. "Is an unshod, broken down donkey worth two thousand five hundred liras?"

"Not having dealt in donkeys, I wouldn't know."

"My friend, I'm not a donkey trader myself either but I know that a donkey isn't worth two thousand five hundred liras."

"Are you upset?"

"You bet I am. If I'm not upset, who will be? Did you ever see a donkey that was worth two thousand five hundred liras?"

"It's been a little over twenty years since I've seen a donkey."

"What I asked you was if a donkey was worth two thousand five hundred liras."

"I don't know what to say. Maybe if he is a donkey that does tricks, he might be worth that much."

"What tricks, my dear sir? This is just a plain donkey. Look, it can't get up and make a speech; it's just a plain old donkey. And it's mangy and worn out, on top of everything else. They sold him to the man for two thousand five hundred liras and the worst of it all, do you know, was that I got him to buy it."

"No! How did all this happen?"

"That's what I came to tell you about. Istanbul University sent me with my wife to America. You know I stayed in America one year."

"I know."

"I met a professor in America and we became friends. He was a lot of help to me. He was very kind. When I got back to Turkey, we continued corresponding. He is a friend of the Turks, a man who likes the Turks very much. In one of his letters he wrote me that a friend of his was coming to Turkey and that this friend was an expert in antique rugs, that he was coming to Turkey to research a book on rugs and asked whether I would assist his friend."

"I wrote back that if his friend the Rug Expert came to Turkey during the university vacation, I would be glad to help him as much as I could. Because the Rug Expert was going to India and Iran to research and coming on to Turkey later, it would be a suitable time for me."

"The Rug Expert came in July. He had my address and phone number from my American professor friend. One day he phoned me from his hotel and I went to the hotel. He was a shrewd fellow. He was an American of German extraction and he probably had some Jewish background too. Perhaps he had been a German Jew and become an American later on."

"He had brought four big trunks filled with rugs, flat weave carpets and saddle bags from the places he had been earlier. He opened his trunks and showed off his antiques. They were very ancient rugs, flat weaves and pieces of saddle bags. He seemed very happy with the pieces he had collected. He told me that they were an enormous treasure. In fact, there was a piece of an old carpet only three inches wide and five or ten inches long that he told me was worth at least thirty thousand dollars but he bragged that he had bought it from an Iranian peasant for one dollar. On top of that, when the poor Iranian peasant took the dinar equivalent of a dollar in his hand he was dumbfounded and uttered prayers of thanksgiving."

"I asked why that old piece of carpet was worth so much money. 'Because,' he said, 'there are eighty knots per cubic centimeter in this rug. It's a masterpiece.' He went on explaining about carpets with a truly sensual longing. Up till now there was only one carpet in the world with as much as one hundred knots per cubic centimeter and it was in I-don't-know which museum and was a wall carpet."

"He showed me a felt piece. 'I got this for fifty cents,' he said and chuckled slyly in his delight. 'This felt rug will be worth at least five thousand dollars,' he said."

"How do you buy these valuable objects so cheap?" I asked him.

"I've been in this business for forty years," he said. "I have my own methods."

Then he told me tactics that made my mouth fall open in amazement. He had published three books on rugs, in addition, he owned one of the finest rug collections in the world.

We started out on a tour of Anatolia. We travelled from province to province and from district to district. He took colored photographs and continually made notes of the rugs in the mosques that he thought were valuable. He bought old saddlebags, rugs, felt weaves and flat weaves from a few people. According to what he told me, what he was buying was worthless compared to what he had bought in India, Afghanistan and Chinese Turkestan. "There *are* some very valuable Turkish rugs but you don't run across them," he said.

We came to a place where they had an archaeological dig. One American and one German archaeological team had each pitched a camp about five or ten kilometers distant from one another and were excavating. They were turning the earth up and had scattered the hills and mountains this way and that like a sheep's wool. They had made flour of the hills and had ground the soil up into powder.

The area they were excavating was about the size of a small town. They had pitched a number of tents. Here lie several civilizations, dating from the tenth century B.C. to the present day, one on top of another, beneath the soil. Not one, but several, cities, palaces, tombs and so on, emerged from beneath the earth.

Because it was such an interesting place, cars full of tourists interested in history and archeology were continually coming and going. You ran into five to ten tourists every couple of kilometers.

Peasants had gathered around the excavation and were selling the tourists the historical and archaeologically valuable pieces of pottery that they had dug up. The tourists were just scrambling to buy them. Even the village children had lined up alongside the road and were selling rings, stones with inscriptions and pieces of broken vases that they had dug up for the tourists. Tiny bare footed boys and girls were running after the tourists, all screaming, "*Van dalir, tuu dalir*".

I thought that since I had come all the way here, I might as well buy myself a souvenir. There was a blond girl who looked only ten years old who had the handle of a vase in her hand and a boy with a blue stone in the shape of a man's head. I thought that the blue stone might be the stone belonging to a ring.

"How much do you want for those, my child?" I said.

The little girl wanted forty liras for the vase handle and the boy wanted fifteen liras for the blue stone in the shape of a head. Now not because I didn't know what they were but just to buy them cheap, I said, "They are too expensive."

The boy and girl started to argue like grownups. They certainly weren't expensive. Their father had dug for days and found them five meters under the ground.

I was about to buy them but my American Rug Expert friend, after telling me that they had neither historical nor archaeological value, said that the situation was the same in every place he had travelled in the East. "It is exactly the same there. The peasants, men, women and children, stop the tourists in the road every place where there are digs that attract tourists. They pass off anything they can get their hands on for an antique."

These sly peasants faked the ancient artifacts so cleverly they even fooled famous archaeologists and swindled them by selling them stuff at high prices. They even sold the shaven carcass of a sheepdog to an American tourist as the mummy of a king. But the imitations that these peasant counterfeiters made were not things to be sneezed at. They were works of great skill and accomplishment, for example the tiny blue stone in the shape of a man's head that I saw in the hand of the child a little while earlier. It's not easy to make things like that.

We were riding in the jeep we had rented. The weather was

very hot. We saw a couple of poplars and a well beside the road. We were going to eat our lunch in the shade. An elderly peasant was stretched out, dozing in the shade of the poplars and a donkey was grazing a little beyond the peasant.

We greeted the peasant and started talking. I was translating into English for the American what the peasant said.

"What do you grow the most of in these villages around here?" I asked.

"'Not a thing," he said. "We used to farm. We grew grain but since they started this digging, it's been twenty years I reckon, the peasants have gotten lazy and now they don't sow anything."

The American said, "It's the same in the other places."

I asked the old man,"Well, how do the peasants get by?"

"Since it's been the style to dig up broken pottery and pieces of stones and such like, the peasants have left their work and they sell whatever they find by digging up the excavation to all those foreigners that pour in."

The American said, "It's the same as in other places."

"Our people here are real lowdown types," the peasant said. "They have sold all our country's treasures to the foreigners. They found such stone columns and tombs that if they could learn their value and sell them, they could found ten more Turkeys... and who are these foreigners we're talking about? They're all of them thieves. They have continually pilfered these antiques that are dug up and smuggled them out. They have built enormous cities in their own countries with the stuff they've stolen. Some of them dug them up and stole them themselves and some of them swindled the peasants out of what they had dug up."

The American said, "It's the same other places."

"Now," he said, "there's not a piece of filth left under the ground to dig up and if there is, it's of no account. The government has woken up now and doesn't let anybody get their hands on anything. If these foreigners steal anything, they steal it from the government because the government is supposed to be selling these things at their right price."

The American said,"Yes, that's the way it is other places."

"So how do the peasants get by now?"

"Well, there's six villages hereabouts. If you go in their houses you won't see so much as a piece of cloth or a glass or a pitcher or a jug. Everybody's house is as empty as last year's bird nest."

"Why?"

"Why do you think? They've sold them to the tourists. There's not a splinter of wood left in their houses. Anything they had, they made into antiques and sold. They buried them in the ground, made them rust and turned them into crumbly antiques. Our people's morals have really gone bad, mister. Yesterday, I caught a little boy trying to steal the beads from my donkey's harness. Once he got his hands on them he would bury them in the ground, you see, and then he was going to dig them up and pass them off for antiques. The girls of an age to get married and living at home have all turned into antique makers. If they get their hands on a piece of stone the size of your finger, they carve and chip it and turn out a piece of art you wouldn't believe. They make medals and ancient money out of donkey shoes."

The American said, "I told you so. It's exactly the same in other places."

I asked the old peasant, "How do you get by? What do you do?"

"I trade in donkeys," he said.

When he said this he drew some water from the well and gave it to his donkey to drink in the trough attached to the well. While the donkey was drinking, the American jumped up and went over to the donkey. The peasant and I were talking.

"Can you make a living in this donkey business?"

"Praise Allah, I have made a living for five years in this business, thank God."

"What do you earn, for example?"

"It all depends on the donkey."

"How long does it take you to sell a donkey?"

"It depends. Sometimes a donkey doesn't sell for three to five months. Sometimes you sell five donkeys in one day."

The American walked over to me. He was very excited.

"Good grief," he said, "do you see that piece of carpet on that donkey?"

The peasant didn't understand because we were talking English.

There was an old, ragged, muddy saddlecloth on the donkey's back.

"You mean that dirty cloth?" I said.

"Oh my goodness," he said, "it's a wonder, a masterpiece. I've been studying that carpet ever since you two started to talk. The colors, the design are amazing and the workmanship is fabulous. It has exactly one hundred and twenty knots per cubic centimeter. Nothing like that has been seen in the world before, it's priceless."

"Do you want to buy it?" I said.

"Yes," he said, "but I don't want the peasant to know that I'm buying the carpet. I know these people here. If you try to buy their old, worn sandals they want a world of money because they think that they are valuable and antiques. What they plan to make off the deal isn't the issue. They are never satisfied however much money you offer them. They keep on raising the price. That's why we don't want to let on to the peasant."

About then the old peasant said, "What is that heathen jabbering about? You two are going 'gobble, gobble, gobble'."

"Nothing," I said, "he just likes it a lot here."

"What is there to like here? There's nothing but naked chalk cliffs."

The American said, "I told you that I had methods for buying cheap, didn't I? Well now I'm going to use one of those methods."

"What?"

"I'm not going to act as though I'm interested in the carpet.

I'm going to buy the donkey. Naturally, since the peasant doesn't know the value of the carpet, he is going to leave the old cloth on the donkey's back when we buy it. Then we'll take the carpet and let the donkey loose a little way down the road. Now, will you tell the peasant that I want to buy the donkey?"

I said to the peasant, "Didn't you want to sell the donkey?"

"Yep, I was going to sell the donkey," he said.

"For instance, how much would you sell this donkey for?"

"Depends on who the buyer is."

"Suppose we were to buy it?"

He laughed.

"Are you having fun with me? What would gentlemen the likes of you do with a donkey?"

"What do you care, man? We want to buy this donkey. What will you sell it for?"

"I told you, didn't I. It depends on the buyer. Is it you that's going to buy it or this heathen?"

"He is."

"What nationality is that guy?"

"American."

"Humh, he's not a foreigner, we can reckon he's one of us. Look here, this donkey is really old and broken down. Tell him this donkey is no good to him."

I told the American.

"Oh good, that means he's going to sell it cheap," he said.

"He doesn't care whether it's old or not."

"It would be a shame to do an American like that. He'll go home and say the Turks swindled him."

I told the American this.

"The Turkish peasants are a very innocent, very honest people," he said. "Anywhere else they would have sold it to me right away. Since he's such a good hearted fellow, I will pay him a lot of money."

I said to the peasant, "The American agrees."

"Yes, but sir," he said, "this donkey will die on the road before it gets to America and anyway this donkey has terrible mange. He's nasty with mange from head to tail."

"What do you care, my friend? The man wants him."

"Allah, Allah. Look, this isn't a female even to be of any use. What is he going to do with this old, mangy donkey?"

"What business is it of yours? Just think about the money. What do you want for this donkey?"

"I'm really curious," the peasant said. "Just ask this American efendi: 'don't they have any donkeys at all in his country?'"

"He's asking, 'Don't you have any donkeys in your country?'"

The American answered after thinking a little, "Tell him we do but we don't have any like this."

I told the peasant.

"Hummh, so he doesn't like American donkeys but he does Turkish donkeys. Well, what can I do? It's not my fault. I told him everything that was wrong with the donkey. I am not about to hurt the feelings of somebody who's come all the way from abroad because of a mangy donkey. I'll sell it."

"How much?"

"For you, ten thousand."

"Whaat? Are you crazy? The finest Arab thoroughbred only brings two or three thousands liras."

"So then what d'you want with the donkey? Let him buy the finest thoroughbred."

When I told the American that the man wanted ten thousand liras, he said, "Didn't I tell you? That's the way these people are. They want lots of money because they think it's valuable. What if we had tried to buy the carpet? He's have wanted a hundred thousand liras then. I could offer him ten thousand liras for the donkey but then he would want fifty thousand when I started to pay him. That's why you have to bargain firmly with them."

I said to the peasant, "Tell the truth. What did you pay for this donkey?"

"I don't tell lies," he said. "Look, I've just washed myself to pray and I'm not about to tell a lie. I bought this donkey for five liras to skin to make sandals with. He's going to die any day now and I'll skin him then. He's not good for anything else."

"Come on, play fair! How can you try to sell a donkey that you paid five liras for for ten thousand liras?"

"Son, I'm not trying to sell it, it's you who are trying to buy. I said it was old and the man said that was all right. I said that it had the mange, he accepted that. I said that it wasn't a female and he still wanted it. I said it wouldn't live another day and he still said 'good'. Oh, I almost forgot...the donkey is lame. Its right leg limps."

"It doesn't matter."

"You see, there's something valuable, something marvelous about this donkey that I don't understand. Otherwise why would this American infidel try to buy a mangy, old jackass and lame too? Isn't that right? Ten thousand, I won't take any less for it!"

I said to the American, "He won't go down any farther. Shall we give him the ten thousand?"

We haggled for two hours. Several times we acted as though we had given up and walked away. He paid no attention. We walked back to him.

"I knew you'd come back," he said.

"How did you know?" I said.

"Who wouldn't know it, my boy? You're come across such bargain of a donkey that you are certainly not going to walk away from it."

I told the driver of the jeep to take the jeep and wait for us a little distance down the road. We were going to let the donkey loose and climb into the jeep.

Anyway, sir, after bickering and bargaining we settled on two thousand five hundred liras. We counted the money out into his hand and the peasant took the saddle cloth and put it on his shoulder and put the donkey's reins in our hands.

"Well, then, use it in good health," he said.

Then he added, "I probably sold my broken down, mangy donkey too cheap but never mind. Use it in good health."

The American was staring at the piece of carpet in the peasant's hand. What were we going to do now?

"My God," he said, "don't let on anything. We'll lead the donkey off a little ways and then come back here. We'll say, 'Oh my goodness, the donkey's back will get cold. Give us the cloth and we'll cover it up.' Be careful that the man doesn't understand that what we are really after is the piece of carpet."

We took the donkey's lead and walked off. I say we walked off just as a manner of speaking because we had a hard time walking. The American pushed from behind and I pulled from in front but the donkey wouldn't budge. The old donkey didn't have the strength to move. If we could only get the carpet away from the peasant, we could have left the donkey and taken off.

We had gone about twenty or thirty paces, pushing and shoving the donkey, when we heard the voice of the peasant calling after us, "Stop, stop, you forgot the donkey's thing."

Oh, if you had only seen how happy the man was that the cloth was following us on its own. The man came running over the hilltop.

"Hey there," he said. "What are you going to tie this donkey to when you get it to America? You didn't even think. You don't buy a donkey without a stake. I can see you're greenhorns."

And we took the iron donkey stake with the ring on the end from his hand.

The American said to me, "Come on, now's the moment to ask for the carpet. But for goodness sake don't give us away. Say, 'Just give that dirty saddle cloth here, will you?'"

I said to the peasant, "This donkey is very sickly. It would be a shame if he caught cold. You had an old cloth on the donkey. Give us the dirty cloth and we'll put it on its back."

"Oh, no," he said. "I can't give the cloth to you. You bought the donkey from me, not the cloth."

"Yes, we bought the donkey. Now let's put the cloth on it. Anyway, it's old and dirty and it's not worth a *para*."

"Yes, it's old and dirty and it's not worth one *para* but I can't give it to you."

"Why?"

"I can't give it to you, Mister. It's an heirloom from my father, that cloth. It's an heirloom handed down from my ancestors and forefathers. I can't give it to you."

I said to the American, "He says that it's an heirloom handed down from his forefathers."

"Ask him what it's good for," he said.

"What good is this dirty piece of cloth to you?" I asked him.

The peasant suddenly became serious, "What do you mean, 'What good is it to me'? I'm going to buy another mangy donkey and put it on his back. If it is my *kismet*, I'll find somebody else interested and, with Allah's assistance, I'll sell it to him too. This cloth has brought me luck, I'm telling you. I gave you the stake for free too. Did I say anything about that?"

"Oh, come on now, let us buy the cloth for a few piasters and cover the animal."

"Now you've done it! Then how will I sell my donkeys? I've been selling worn out, mangy donkeys for five years now thanks to this cloth. Goodby to you now. Use it in good health."

I was afraid the American was going to have a heart attack. I took him by the arm.

After a few steps, the peasant shouted from a distance,

"If you are going to let that donkey loose, please don't take him a far ways off, so you won't wear yourselves out."

We let the donkey loose there, on the spot and walked back to the jeep.

The American Rug Expert said, "Now *this* is something that doesn't go on anywhere else. It's never happened to me before. Everything is the same as elsewhere here, but this is a different sort of a ploy."

We got into the jeep. He still had the stake in his hand. He couldn't throw it away.

"What are you going to do with that iron stake?" I said.

"I am going to add this stake to my rug collection as a souvenir," he said. "This stake is valuable. We got it cheap at two thousand five hundred."

"You see? I'm disgraced before the world. Shame on me."

He kept on repeating, "I'm disgraced" over and over again and kept slapping his forehead with his hand.

[Translator's note: The phrase *kazík yemek*, literally "to eat the stake (be impaled)," which originally referred to a form of capital punishment used by the Ottomans, now means "to be swindled" in contemporary slang. The narrator seems to feel personal shame because the American Rug Expert, who was his guest and under his protection, is going to add the iron *kazík* he "ate" in Turkey in his collection in America.]

Number Fifteen

("Onbeş Numara" from *İnsanlar Uyanıyor,* 1972)

I had boarded the Izmit bus. I was going to Bayramoglu.
Bayramoglŭ is sixty kilometers from Kadıköy.

It was time to leave but the bus didn't move. When the
passengers started to murmur, someone on the bus said, "Two
passengers haven't gotten here yet. Let's wait a little longer."

The man who had said this stuck his head out of the bus
door and started yelling the seat numbers of the two passengers who hadn't arrived, "Number fifteeen! Number twenty-
oneee!"

Since he was busying himself with the latecomers, he must
be some sort of company employee, either the driver or the
driver's helper or the ticket taker.

"Number twenty-oneee!"

A big, hulking man came, huffing and puffing, a basket in
one hand, a sack in the other, the nape of his neck as red as a
tomato and as puffed up as a tea cake. He climbed aboard the
bus and sat in seat number twenty-one.

The man who had yelled the numbers of the empty seats
started to scold him, saying, "Why don't you get on in time and
not keep all these passengers waiting?"

But when the ruddy man with the puffy neck, turning around with his whole body because he couldn't turn just his thick neck, shot back gruffly, "What's it to you, damn it all? What are you jabbering about?" the other got quiet as a mouse but he was very angry. To vent his anger, he began to shout towards the square in an even higher voice, the number of the remaining empty seat,

"Number fifteeen! Number fifteeen! Look here, number fifteen! Where are you, damn it all, number fifteeen?"

His voice resounded through the square.

One of the passengers said, "Come on, let the bus leave!"

The man who had been yelling said to the passenger, "It's only been three minutes. What difference would it make if we waited another couple of minutes?" Then he leaned out of the bus door and continued shouting towards the square, "Number fifteeen! Hey there, number fifteeen!"

The driver took his seat and started the engine, so then the man who had been yelling wasn't the bus driver. The bus sat there rattling while the man shouted fit to burst his lungs, "Number fifteeen!"

The front door was closed. The bus started to move. We were just about to leave when a man came flying up in total confusion and barely threw himself into the bus. Because the bus was already moving he staggered along looking for his place and sat in seat number fifteen which was empty. His chest was heaving like a bellows and he was all out of breath.

The man who had been yelling the seat numbers just a little while before started to scold the late passenger, "Why don't you get on board on time and not make all these people wait?"

The belated passenger said ashamedly, "You're right, sorry."

But then the other one became even more contrary.

"What'd you mean 'sorry'? After all these passengers waited for you, now you say you're 'sorry'!"

"Oh my God, I don't know what more I can say. I beg your pardon."

"What right do you think you have to make us wait?"

The passenger, who was scrunched down in seat fifteen, said in a teary voice, "Of course, I had no right. It was a shame. It was a terrible shame."

"When you buy your ticket, you don't go wandering off from the bus."

"I swear to God, it's not something that I ever do. I have always been a careful, a very cautious person. I always go to the vehicle I'm traveling on a long while before departure time."

"We waited for you for five minutes, damn it."

"Believe me, this is the first time it's ever happened."

"The fault is ours for having waited so long for you."

"I don't know what to say. You are right."

"The bus should have left then, you would have come to your senses."

The other travelers were silent. They were listening to the conversation of the passenger in seat number fifteen and the man in the rear space of the bus. The delayed passenger was a thin, bespectacled gentleman who looked about fifty years old. However much he humbled himself, pouring out his apologies for having kept us waiting, the other crowed the louder, raising his tone higher and higher:

"They shouldn't let your kind ride on a bus. There shouldn't be a second's delay. When the time comes, the bus should just leave."

"You are so right but what can I do, it's happened already. I said, didn't I, this is the first time it's happened to me? Anything you say is justified."

"I strained my voice shouting, 'Number fifteen, number fifteen'."

"I don't know how I came to be late; I can't say."

"I yelled and yelled but the fellow was nowhere to be found."

"My God, you can say anything to me you want."

The ticket-taker was checking our tickets so then the man who was doing the screaming wasn't the ticket-taker. He might be the assistant to the driver but the driver's assistant was distributing bottles of water to the passengers who wanted them. What then? Maybe he was the owner of the bus.

We had gone more or less thirty kilometers and passed Tuzla. The man whose connection with the bus I hadn't been able to figure out was still scolding the late arrival without a pause and the passenger was still trying to defend himself, squirming and begging pardon.

"Everybody has some business to take care of. You don't keep this many people waiting, damn it. Shame on you."

"I wish I had never gone off. I wish I had had a broken leg so I wouldn't have left the bus."

"When you buy your ticket, you go and sit in your seat, mister."

"All together I only made you wait five little minutes."

"Oh my goodness, sir. Just five minutes, damn it all. Oh no, we should have waited for your lordship a week."

"What's done is done. What more can I do?"

"Now he says, 'What's done is done'. You should be ashamed of yourself, by God. Look here, the least anybody could do is be ashamed and keep his mouth shut."

The passenger who had shrunk into his seat remained silent but the other one had raised his voice to a shout:

"If you can't make it, you should buy a ticket for the next bus."

He waited a while for the answer. When there was none,

"Now he won't talk, look at that. A human being would say he was sorry. People like that drive you crazy, I swear to God."

As the bus was turning down the side road to Bayramoğlu, the puffy passenger with the thick red neck sitting in seat number twenty-one shouted at the man who had been yelling for an hour, "What are you on this bus anyways? Who'n hell are you?"

The shouting man suddenly turned shy.

"Me? Who, me? Oh, nobody. I'm a passenger on the bus," he said.

The bus stopped on the Bayramoglu side road and I got out. I was so curious about what happened afterwards on that bus that I was sorry I had gotten off.

Hamdi the Elephant

("Fil Hamdi" from *Fil Hamdi,* 1977)

This is how they caught Hamdi the Elephant.
This was the telegram that the Istanbul Police Department
sent all the provincial police departments,

> *"A dangerous, convicted con artist, alias 'Hamdi*
> *the Elephant', thirty-five years old, tall, weighing two*
> *hundred kilos, brown hair, three teeth missing, upper*
> *molar filled, lower canine gold-plated, striped brown*
> *suit, partly bald, round face, brown eyes, has escaped*
> *from the custody of two of our policemen by exploiting*
> *their dozing off to sleep after having carefully guarded*
> *the guard box they were sitting in for three days and*
> *nights. It has definitely been established as the conclu-*
> *sion of all our investigations, proceedings and re-*
> *searches that Hamdi the Elephant has escaped. In the*
> *event that he should stop by one of the provincial or*
> *district police stations to ask for some directions or the*
> *address of a policeman, please tell him not to leave us*
> *wondering any longer but to turn himself in at the*
> *Istanbul Police Department at his earliest convenience.*
> *Please find a photograph of the dangerous felon Hamdi*
> *the Elephant enclosed."*

In a provincial railroad station, two policemen were talking to one another.

"Ramazan, my brother, that fellow over there drinking *salep* is Hamdi the Elephant for certain."

"Huh, looks like him alright. Let's have a look at that picture."

He pulled out the picture and showed it to his friend.

"That's not him, Ramazan, by goodness, that's you!"

"Huh? Oh, I had it taken over the holidays. How is it?"

""It's alright but why didn't you smile a little? Come on and let's find Hamdi the Elephant's picture."

Ramazan pulled a wad of pictures out of his pocket and shuffled through them.

"That's my kid's picture. This one was taken when I was in the army...Who's this one, Mahmut?'

"Him? Oh, that's Dopehead Ali, the heroin smuggler."

"And this is Suphi, the sneak hotel thief. These pictures are all mixed up. Hey, find us that Hamdi the Elephant."

Mahmut and Ramazan sorted through the pictures (and they looked for Hamdi the Elephant's picture).

"Hurry it up, Mahmut. That guy has drunk his *salep*. He's getting ready to leave."

"See how he's looking all around."

"I found it. This is the picture. That's it! He's the one."

They went up to the suspect.

"Stop right there, buddy."

They looked first at the picture, then at the man's face.

"Stand sideways."

"Say, Ramazan, this doesn't look like him."

"Let's let His Honor the Superintendent have a look at him. Maybe he'll see some resemblance."

"Come on, buddy. We're going to the police station."

* * *

Two policemen were talking in the marketplace of a country town.

"Shükrü, my friend, isn't it a shame? We chase all over the place from morning to night and we haven't caught Hamdi the Elephant yet."

"Could he be that man?"

"Maybe it's him. Let's ask him."

They went up to the man.

"Mister, what's your name."

"Mustafa."

They whisper into one another's ears, "He says it's 'Mustafa'."

"Well, he isn't about to say he's 'Hamdi'...He's hiding his real name."

"He'll make a fool of us if we let him."

"Mister, would you please come with us..."

* * *

Two policemen were talking to one another in a country coffeehouse.

"I caught three Hamdi the Elephants yesterday, but my Superintendent didn't like a single one."

"Well, I don't care if he *is* our Superintendent. He's darned hard to please."

"Shush...Quiet down. Look at that guy over there drinking tea."

"Why, it's him. He's the one."

"But that paper that came says he's fat. This guy is thin, like a skeleton."

"Buddy, he's lost weight. You think it's easy to escape from jail?"

"Okay, but this one is dark-haired. Hamdi the Elephant is supposed to be a blond."

"Wandering around the countryside must have changed his complexion."

"You're right but this one has lots of hair and the paper says that Hamdi the Elephant has lost most of his."

"Oh, well, that may be. Maybe he's stuck a wig on his head for a disguise."

"What are we waiting for? Let's arrest him."

They approached the man.

"What's your name?"

"Hamdi."

They glanced at one another meaningfully and smiled.

"Come along to the police station...move."

"What's going on? What's the matter?"

"Don't ask so many questions. You'll find out at the police station."

* * *

Two policemen arrested a man walking along the one or two kilometers of asphalt road such as a provincial capital has.

"Open your mouth."

"What for? There's nothing in my mouth."

"Open it, if there's nothing in it."

The man opened his mouth. Both looked at his teeth at the same time.

One policeman asked the other, "Look at that paper. How many of his teeth are missing?"

The other one looked at the paper.

"'Three canines missing, a filled molar in the jaw and a gold-plated canine in his lower left jaw.'"

The policeman counted the man's teeth.

"One, two three...Don't move, damn it. You'll mix me up. One, two three...four, five.'"

"Twenty-four teeth. He's got twenty-four teeth."

"Twenty-four? How many is he missing? You know how many teeth he's missing?"

"Eight."

"He must have had them pulled. He's had them pulled to wipe out the evidence."

"My teeth are artificial. I don't have any of my own teeth left. In fact, I broke four of my teeth eating roast corn."

"In that paper does it say whether or not the teeth are artificial?"

"It doesn't say. They forgot to put that in. But he's the one, the very one. Look, his canine is gold-plated. Come along with us, mister."

"Where to?"

"To the police station. March!"

* * *

Every day hundreds of wires were coming in to the Istanbul Police Department from the provincial police departments.

> *"In reference to telegram numbered such and such and dated such and such:"*
>
> *"Fourteen Hamdi the Elephants wearing striped, brown clothes, eight of them having a gold-plated canine tooth, have been arrested in our province. We respectfully inquire whether this amount is sufficient and whether the search should be continued."*
>
> *"In response to the telegram bearing such and such a date:"*
>
> *"Two dozen Hamdi the Elephants, ranging in weight from 180 to 220 kilos arrested in this province. Stop. Difference in weights is undoubtedly caused by inaccuracy in scales, since all have brown eyes. Stop. No doubt they are Hamdi the Elephant. Stop. Sending Hamdi the Elephants. Stop. If any have been overlooked, request that they also be sought with great care and sent here, one by one. Stop."*

Here is the wire the Istanbul Police Department sent to the provincial police departments:

> *"Existing Hamdi the Elephants have been deemed sufficient because we no longer have any place to put them. Stop. Until you receive another order, request that you temporarily stop arresting and searching for Hamdis. Stop."*

Note: Hamdi the Elephant, the absconder, *was* arrested.

The Neutron Bomb Will Save Civilization

("Nötron Bombası Uygarlığı Kurtaracaktır" from
Sanat Dergisi, March 6, 1978)

We have learned a fearful lesson from the First and the
Second World War that followed it. We have seen how at the
end of both wars the historical monuments which were the
great works of civilization, the great buildings, the houses of
worship, the bridges, the museums which honor our civilization and the factories which are both the product and crea-
tions of our technical progress, all the school houses and
university buildings, the libraries which guard all the historical documents of civilization and all the great cities, were
destroyed and annihilated. These things which had been destroyed were the very essence of civilization itself.

The reconstruction, restoration and rebuilding of these
monuments of civilization destroyed in the First and Second
World Wars was very difficult and expensive.

Great efforts and research have been expended to find an-
swers to this difficulty. A weapon must be constructed that
would kill the enemy but which would not harm the stones,
concrete, soil, iron and cement. Indeed, concrete, iron or stones
have no enemies.

What have the poor stones, the concrete, the iron and the wood or the monuments of civilization, ever done to us that we should destroy them? As a result of all this research, they succeeded in discovering the neutron bomb. We can thus see that the neutron bomb is a weapon which will save and protect our civilization and is the greatest wonder of our age. Can you think, it is difficult to conceive of it, that the neutron bomb which will leak through all the nooks and crannies of the buildings which are the monuments of civilization and destroy every living thing in them, will not damage in the least the whitewash of those buildings, the paint on the doors and windows, the carpets on the floors, the lace on the curtains, the gilded mirror frames, the wallpaper or the lacquer on the furniture and will not even make the windows rattle? Can you conceive of a more humane or civilized weapon? And after such a war, we who remain alive will use at our pleasure the totally empty cities saved from all damage, the apartments with no one in them, furnished too, the ships in the deserted harbors, the museums and schools and universities and libraries without men. There will only remain a small cleaning job for the people who will have become the possessors of these relics of civilization: that will be to gather together and dispose of the refuse left over from the people, from the human cadavers and the piles of bones and ashes left by the cadavers and to purify our beautiful world adorned with the works of civilization.

Who can oppose the use of the neutron bomb, the greatest miracle of our age which will save civilization, because it kills people? We must not forget: what possible use is a bomb which neither kills people nor destroys buildings? Some people compare a bomb with a spray gun to kill bugs. The neutron bomb is not a spray gun for flies!

The number killed in both World Wars was around sixty million. If those sixty million had not died, their descendants would have increased over the last thirty years and today they would be at least two hundred million. If we were to add two hundred million to this world into which we can barely squeeze as it is, our world would become completely unlivable.

In these days, it is not from a dearth of people what we suffer; on the contrary, there are more people that we want or know what to do with in our world.

As we know, to sustain world market prices, surplus agricultural produce such as grain, potatoes and coffee are destroyed by being thrown into the sea or burned. It is for this reason that for example in agricultural planning, sometimes farmers are paid for the wheat they did not sow that year, just as if they had cultivated and reaped that wheat. Just because people who exceed the world's requirements are destroyed just like agricultural produce such as potatoes, grain, coffee and so forth are destroyed by burning in order not to undercut the prices of the world market, is no reason for propaganda to be made against us. Therefore, the decrease of the number of mankind by natural means in wars is the most intelligent and suitable proposition for keeping the world population in balance.

All over the world today, there is an effort to prevent increase of population. It is for this reason in fact that population planning and population limitation is being carried out and that even people's sexual desires are being restrained and in fact people are being sterilized in some places. While the situation is thus, it shows lack of understanding of what civilization consists of to represent the neutrons bomb's ability to kill people while not damaging iron, stone, wood, concrete, cloth, lace and velvet, as some sort of deficiency or as a fault. Man is a sum of numbers consisting of his shirt size, his shoe number, his phone number, his insurance number, his house number, his gas, electricity and water meter numbers, the numbers of the busses, trolleys and streetcars he rides on and great many other numbers as well. So then, let us compare figures: sixty million men died in the First and Second World Wars. If contemporary civilization should feel that it needed sixty million people, it would carry out population planning to obtain sixty million more people in the same way that it would plant wheat if more wheat were needed. It is a much easier and, by the way, a more agreeable job to make children than to build the buildings which are the monuments of civilization, as every man and woman who had experimented in this field knows.

If a museum collapses we make another museum. If sixty million people die, we can make sixty million more and...brand new and fresh as daisies.

It is truly hard to understand what the people who are opposed to the neutron bomb want. That is, do they absolutely want the museums, scientific laboratories, monuments, houses of worship, schools and university buildings, libraries and factories destroyed together with the people the neutron bomb kills?

The opponents of the neutron bomb forget this: those who die by the explosion of the neutron bomb will never be we civilized men who are the custodians of civilization.

How They Loved the Old Man

("Ne çok Seviyorlardı Yaşlı Adamı" from *Yetmiş Yaşım Merhaba,* 1984)

The old man's family was a large one. His next of kin were his two daughters and his three sons. They were all married and had children. He had a bunch of grandchildren and everyone was employed and earning his living. Some of his children lived in the same city, some in other cities and one was in Germany.

He also had two sisters and one brother. One of his brothers had settled in Australia.

Apart from his children and brothers, the old man had many relatives in the second degree, close and distant. He didn't even know most of them.

He had retired twenty years ago. He had a great many acquaintances and friends.

It had been fifteen years since he had left his wife and from that time he had lived alone. His loneliness increased a little every day. The day came when the old man began to feel as though he were a tiny grain of sand in a limitless sand dune of loneliness, a grain of sand that had been blown all alone through the air from afar off, and that there wasn't another grain of sand near him or even in his proximity.

He had dozens of sons, daughters and grandchildren but not one of them knocked on his door. Some of them contented themselves with dropping in on four or five holidays but the others never came. They didn't even write very many letters. If it occurred to them, some of them might send him a greeting card on a holiday or on the New Year but most of them didn't even do that much.

The old man didn't complain because his children and grandchildren didn't visit him or ask after him, didn't come to his house, didn't concern themselves with him and didn't write to him. He thought, "Who knows what problems they have, what troubles they have in this life?" so that they couldn't find time to concern themselves with him. He thought the same for his close and distant relatives. It was not as if they didn't want to come and see him. They must want to but they can't find a chance with all the difficulties they must have in life. Even his sisters and brother had stopped coming long ago and they didn't even communicate with him. It must mean that they can't even find the time to write him a letter. His friends and acquaintances were the same. Who could say what problems they too had?

Whereas, in former times, the old man's house had been like a continual party, filled with merrymaking day and night. His house had never lacked for children, grandchildren, brothers and sisters, nieces and nephews, close relatives, distant relatives, acquaintances and friends. Later on, as the years went by, slowly they all of them stopped coming.

At first the old man thought that he had given reason for their avoiding him. Because he was the eldest in the family, they should have come to see him but perhaps the old man should have been the one to go to them or write them letters.

And so he did. But still nobody came to see him or asked about him. It was then that the old man understood that he had to accept his loneliness as a condition of being old and concede the naturalness of a man's being alone at his age. It must mean that this was the way things were after this age.

As far as being old was concerned, he was old but he didn't

show his age at all. He was healthy and full of life. Many people when they first met him and he told them couldn't believe his age. He thought up things to do, never sat idle and didn't even know how the time had passed.

While the days were thus flowing by, an unexpected discovery, one he had never before made, suddenly changed the course of his life. This unexpected discovery was a young girl. She was beautiful, attractive, intelligent, lovable, warm and congenial. He met this young girl in the house of a friend his own age. In order not to appear amorous towards the young girl, who was less than half his age, he even acted a little cold in response to the girl's attentions. He had enough intelligence to see the absurdity of such a relationship. Yes, he was old but he was not in his dotage. Despite all this, his struggle not to form a sentimental relationship with the girl and his understanding of the unsuitability of such a relationship did not help because that beautiful young girl began to visit his house frequently and somehow made her feelings for the old man plain with her every movement. However much the old man resisted, pretending at first not to understand, in the end he yielded to the current of life. He was old but he had not turned his back altogether on life's pleasures. Didn't people say that men were only as old as they felt, not as they looked? After all, he was not the first old man on this earth to love a girl who was much younger than himself. On top of everything, his desire wasn't one-sided, either.

Color, light, savor had come into the old man's life. He floated in a world of happiness such as he had never known till then. This must mean that there was this side to life also. If it weren't for this girl, he would have left this world without having experienced that which he truly should have.

Both of them knew that their romantic relationship didn't correspond to normal custom, that it was not even considered normal, but they didn't deceive either one another or themselves. They just loved each other.

Only a month and a half after this romantic relationship had started, another change took place in the old man's life.

Children, grandchildren, close and distant relations, colleagues, friends, even nodding acquaintances and, of all things, people of whom he could remember neither the names nor where he had met them, began to concern themselves with the old man's life, with his health, with his welfare, in short, with everything about him. The first person to show an interest was the friend of his own age in whose house he had met his beloved, the young girl. This friend had not come to his house since his romance with the young girl had started but he frequently sent messages like this through other people:

"I want what is best for him. It's just not right for a man that age to be friends with such a young girl. He can't keep up with a young girl and, God help us, he may just pop off."

"Then there is the moral aspect of the thing. He met the girl in my house. That puts me in a difficult position. I mean, am I a what-do-you-call-it?"

Early one morning his eldest daughter who was forty-eight and who hadn't darkened his door in years came to his house and said this:

"Papa, you can't know how much I love you. You must believe that I think about you all the time. According to what I hear, you are running around with a very young girl. It's not at all right for a man your age."

A few days later, his middle son came and said this:

"Father, you have made the whole family miserable. Recently we met and talked over your relationship with that young girl and the way you've been lately. In the end we came to this conclusion: you much end this relationship! We are very embarrassed in front of everyone. Everyone has started to look at us in the oddest way."

The old man asked why the last thing he had heard from him was a holiday card three years ago and why he hadn't contacted him since. The son said, "Everything was normal then. Thank goodness, there was nothing to worry me and make me check up on you."

His son in Germany was the one he liked and valued the most. Although he hadn't gotten a letter from him and hadn't had an answer to his letters for a long time, about this time he received a letter from him. His son had written him a poison pen letter. He, after writing his father how much he loved him, gave him lengthy admonitions. As far away as Germany he had heard that his father was having an affair with a young girl. This business was causing the family to lose its honor. What was more important was that who could tell with what ulterior motive and for what personal gains that young girl had entered into this pretended romantic affair with his father.

The old man read this letter several times and was very shaken by it. However it happened, the young girl read the letter which he had left lying out and that night her eyes were swollen from crying. The young girl said, "Oh, how happy I would be if I could wake up in the morning and be thirty years older."

The child who scolded him the most severely was his forty year old youngest daughter who hadn't visited him for a very long time. She bawled at the top of her voice:

"Shame on you, father. Use your head! Do you want to die or what?"

And now his grandchildren who were all young men and women, started coming frequently to their grandfather's house. They tried their best to protect their grandfather from the young girl and to keep them from being alone together. The old man didn't know one of the granddaughters and one of the grandsons at all. In fact, the first time they came, he asked who they were because he had only seen these two grandchildren once when one of them was in swaddling clothes and the other one was being nursed by her mother and she was cooing and billing. This was the first time since then that they had visited their grandfather.

His divorced wife who hadn't contacted him for fifteen years said, in brief, in the letters that she sent the old man one after the other:

"Whatever may have happened, we lived as husband and wife for six years. For that reason, I don't wish you ill and want your welfare. As far as I know, you are an intelligent, logical man. How could you get involved with a girl the age of your granddaughter? It's bad for your health, before everything else. It is the duty of everyone who cares about you to hinder this improper relationship."

His ex-wife who hadn't contacted him in fifteen years, gave examples of acquaintances who had died because they had married young women. For example, so and so had died of heart failure while he was in bed with a woman thirty-five years younger than he. And on top of that, everybody had seen his corpse stark naked in the bed. And what about so and so? He wasn't even able to die. He had a stroke while he was in a young woman's embrace and suffered on for years. His ex-wife gave any number of such instances in her letters.

Not just his children and grandchildren but even his more distant relatives began to inquire about him and come to his house and those who could not come, started to phone him. A relative his own age, after expounding at great length the dangers of having an affair with such a young girl, asked these questions, while spraying him with the saliva which he couldn't hold in his mouth and making clicking sounds with his tongue against his palate as though he were tasting something sweet, "Is the girl beautiful, at least? I heard she was beautiful, is that right? Huh?"

"How old is she? If you have a picture, let me have a look if nothing else."

"How long has this business been going on? How did it happen, the first time? Go on, tell me, old fellow."

About this time, his brothers who he hadn't seen in years, began to concern themselves with the old man's health, his honor and his life and become involved with him. Even his younger brother with whom he had been on bad terms for years, popped into his house one day and said:

"Never mind the rest. We are brothers. I mean, I have to think of you as my big brother and protect you. Everybody is talking about you. Just listen to what people are saying about you. Then you have to think about your health.'

The brother who had settled in Australia and who he hadn't heard from in years sent him a letter. In the letter which began "Dearest Older Brother," he wrote that he had received very distressing news, that unfortunately he had learned that this news was the truth and that the news was that he was having an affair with a very young girl and that kind of relationship meant death and concluded the letter thus:

"We still need you, dear older brother. Therefore, I and all those who love you are waiting for you to make us happy with the news that you have ended this improper relationship."

His friends who hadn't worried themselves over him for who knows how long, now never left the old man alone for a minute. They took him under their protection. In particular, one schoolmate, relying on their intimacy, said:

"Are you crazy? Everybody but you will have fun with a girl that age. Do you want to turn into a pimp at your age? Your friends who care about you won't allow it. You have to stop seeing this girl right away."

Although, even after he had spoken so positively, he tried, drooling as he spoke, to learn how far the relationship with the girl had gone, he could get nothing out of his friend.

And another friend expressed his opposition to the relationship by muttering, "Why, you've gone wild in your old age! Even if I said that you were going through male menopause, you're much too old for that."

But the ones who were the most angry at the old man on account of his young sweetheart were the wives of his friends who were his own age. Almost all of these women were either aging or elderly females who had long since passed middle age. They were afraid that their own husbands would follow the old man's example and take a young sweetheart but because they couldn't openly disclose their fear, they unceasingly manufactured gossip about the old man and his young sweetheart. Because the continual flow of people coming and going at the old man's house made him uncomfortable, he started going out with his young sweetheart to the countryside, to parks, open air cafes and such places. One night, in a cafe, a married woman whom he felt had wanted to get close to him but whom he hadn't encouraged, tried to mock them by saying, "Is this beautiful young lady your daughter?" but the old man had answered her back, "No, my granddaughter."

Because the old man understood the reason behind this derision, he didn't rave and rant, "What business is it of yours?" but merely smiled and went about his business. As far as the young girl was concerned, she didn't even pay attention to these things.

"Other people don't concern me. I love you. I don't care about anything else," she said.

Till now, the old man could never have imagined the happiness he was experiencing.

But if they could talk and behave this way to him, who knew how they behaved and how they talked to his beloved? He understood what sufferings the young girl must be experiencing. Even when the two of them were together, they made the young girl uncomfortable.

If a couple the old man knew happened to see them together somewhere in the early hours of the evening, they would say something like this, supposedly to protect the old man, "Oh, this is no good! Don't deprive an old man of his sleep at this hour of night. He should be in bed asleep at this hour."

If he should drink a glass of liquor with the young girl some place and an acquaintance see them, he would say to the young girl, "I ask you, should a man this age be encouraged to drink this much? God help us, afterward..."

Since for the first time he had begun to experience happiness with this young girl, how many people had surfaced who wanted to protect the old man, who loved him, who concerned themselves with his health and welfare? Now that the old man was happy for the first time in his life, how many people who hadn't concerned themselves with him, who hadn't knocked on his door, who hadn't darkened his threshold for long years, had been transformed into his guardian angels?

One day the old man said to his beloved, the young girl, "I

have found happiness with you for the first and only time in my life but I see that all these unhappy people will never let us live out our happiness."

The young girl laid her head on her elderly lover's breast and she wept for a long time, loudly sobbing at first, and then silently. These tears showed that all those loveless people had finally conquered. The old man and the young girl parted on that day in great pain and sorrow.

The old man now shut himself up in his house as he used to and withdrew into his shell. Now his sons, daughters, grandchildren, his ex-wife, close and distant relatives, friends, colleagues and acquaintances were all content and not a single one of them asked about the old man, came to his house, wrote him a letter or a card because, now that they had rescued him from happiness, they themselves had found their own contentment. It was then that the old man knew that he was truly old. He hadn't grown old in seventy years but he had aged seventy years in those two months.

What Happened to the Privy of the Forty Stairs?

("Kırk Basamaklı Hela ne oldu"
from *Nah Kalkınırız*, 1988)

He is everything you could expect from one of our country's intellectuals. He has advanced ideas, is democratic, humanitarian. You could say that there was nothing abnormal about him. What is unusual is that in a couple of years, my friend will turn ninety. Even if a man has not become a reactionary by that age, it would be perfectly normal if he were a conservative who longed for the past saying, "Where are those tuna fish we used to get in my day?" So the unusual thing about my friend was that in advanced thinking, he outdid many young people and this was the cause of my friendship. He lives in one of our South-Eastern provinces. He has village roots and he is from a line of rural landowners but he is one of our progressive intellectuals of the kind that is rarely met. So, while he is looked upon rather askance in his own circle, because he comes from an established family and because of his advanced age, he is respected by that circle. It also happens that he has used his age as a device to gain authority and respect in that circle. For example, he feels he has the right to get angry and shout whenever he wants to, where he wants to and at who-

183

ever he wants to. The people around him have accepted this as his right and treat it as normal and, as he ages, his brusqueness increases.

A few years ago, he invited me to be his guest in the South-Eastern town where he lives. He never used to tire of describing the historic structures and the monumental treasures of the town where he lived. He used to describe the inns, mosques, baths, bridges and the ancient cisterns of his town in such detail and such glowing terms that I would be astounded at his profound knowledge. He used to repeat his invitation every time he came to Istanbul. Once in a while he would call me on the phone and tell me how cross he was with me because I hadn't come.

However sincerely I promised to accept my aged and irritable friend's kind invitations, I never could go on account of my work.

Finally, the opportunity came and I determined to go and see the archaeological remains and the historic buildings of that South-Eastern town that my friend never tired of describing to me. When I arrived after a tiring journey, my friend showed me most uncommon hospitality.

I was to have stayed in the town for five days. The evening I got there, my friend decided on four days' sightseeing. Everyday, morning and afternoon, we were to tour the city's singular historic buildings, mosques, churches, monasteries, bridges and caravansaries. According to my friend, even if we were to tour the place not for four but for forty days, we could never see all the sights but we still would just try and see the most important ones anyway. My elderly friend was already experiencing the excitement of seeing those places as he planned our tour that night in his home. Unable to contain himself, he explained the places we were to visit in the morning and I memorized the names of those places: the almshouse of Silahtar Omer Pasha, the Inn of the Shops, the Cut-off Mosque, the Inn of the Chain, the Clock Tower, the Tomb of Zullu Baba, the Bridge of the Three Holes. . . How many things there were to see. I too got enthusiastic as I listened.

We took breakfast in the morning. I was curious. I wanted to see these historic places as soon as possible. I got into the automobile waiting in front of the house.

My host with his snow-white hair, beard, eyebrows and mustache, condescendingly ordered the driver, "To the bazaar!" with his usual frowning, grim expression befitting a descendent of a dynasty of village landholders.

On the way, softening his tone of voice especially for my benefit, my host started to inform me about the Inn of the Shops which we were going to see in the Bazaar. It had been built four hundred years ago. It was itself an Ottoman structure built on the site of where there were supposed to have been altars left over from the Eastern Roman Empire. Later, Husraw II, called also Kaykavus, the Sassanian King, destroyed the altars and built winter quarters for his troops in their place and then when the Abbasids came. . . What detailed, what profound knowledge . . . It was more than you could hold in your memory. He explained the whole history of the Inn of the Shops which we were soon going to see in the Bazaar. The plan, how many rooms it had and how many cellars. It even had a fountain on top of its well that art connoisseurs had come all the way from America and Europe to photograph.

The driver stopped the car and we got out. We were swallowed up by such a crowd that it was as though we had sunk into a swamp and there was no hope of extricating ourselves. My elderly friend stood looking around in total confusion. It was as though he found himself in a strange place he had never been before in his life. In the local dialect which he had never lost and which suited him very well, he muttered to himself, "Ahaaa, where is this? Where is this?"

We were being shoved and pushed this way and that by the crowd and my friend was extremely worried that I might be swept away by the crowd. He roared at the driver, "Damn it all, son, where is the Inn of the Shops?"

The driver looked as us completely uncomprehending and answered the question with another question.

"Where'd you say, gran'dad?"

My host repeated in a loud voice, "The Inn of the Shops, confound it, sonny, the Inn of the Shops."

"Dunno, gran'dad."

Losing all hope in the driver, he seized someone out of the crowd and, pulling him by the arm, he asked, "Look here, mister, where did the Inn of the Shops go to?"

"Whaaaat?"

He asked this sharply of vendors with stands, strolling vendors with push carts, shopkeepers, as though everybody should definitely know. "What happened to the Inn of the Shops? Where'd the Inn of the Shops go off to?"

He got responses like these:

"Whaat?"

"Huh?"

"Which inn?"

"Where'd ya say? Where's that?"

My friend gave up trying to find the Inn of the Shops. He understood that not just he himself but nobody else could find the Inn of the Shops. The Inn of the Shops, so famous at one time and the pride of all the inhabitants of the town, had long ago vanished, Because he hadn't been able to show his guest the Inn of the Shops which he had so extravagantly praised, he said, partly in shame and partly with sadness, "They must have knocked down that big old Inn! Woe is me. . . Blast their souls."

He softened and politely modulated his angry tone and said to me, "Come on, let's go to the Silahtar Omer Pasha's Almshouse.

The Almshouse? Almshouse, Almshouse, that right? Where is this Almshouse at, gran'dad?" the driver asked, stammering for fear of his wrath.

My old friend's white eye brows began to work up and down. He went into a temper tantrum.

"God damn it all. . . and you supposed to be a local man! Shame on you. . . you ought to be ashamed of yourself. Is there anybody who hasn't heard of the great Almshouse? The great big Almshouse? If you asked a little baby, it would know. How many Almshouses are there, anyway? Our Silahtar Omer Pasha's Almshouse!"

He told the driver how to get to the Almshouse. The driver pushed his way through the swamp of people, blowing the horn for all he was worth. He set out on the road. My beloved friend began to forget the shame and embarrassment he had felt at not being able to find the Inn by explaining the Almshouse of Silahtar Omer Pasha. I don't believe that Silahtar Omer Pasha himself who had the Almshouse built could have known as many things about the Almshouse. Every day, two meals were distributed to the one thousand poor people. There were three kinds of food at every meal and every day the food was different. The expenses of the Almshouse were covered by the income from the shops which Omer Pasha had built in the Bazaar and, according to foreign experts, this Covered Bazaar was, though small, the most pleasant of all the covered bazaars of the East. As he explained this, he was more and more carried away by his enthusiasm. After we had toured the Almshouse, we would tour the Covered Bazaar.

While he was still in the middle of his explanation, he shouted at the driver, "Where you going? Stop! The Almshouse should be here!"

We were jolted when the driver slammed on the brakes in his fright. We got out of the car. My aged friend raised his head and looked and looked at the enormous office building, he raised his head so high that he had to take hold of his hat so that it wouldn't fall off of his head. He stood there for a while, with his head raised, looking upwards. It was as though he would never lower his head to look at the earth, if he could have avoided it. Then, suddenly, as though he were demanding payment of a debt from him, he grabbed a passer-by by the arms and shouted at him, "Damn it, where is Silahtar Omer Pasha's Almshouse?"

The man who wore peasant dress, said fearfully and with an Arabic accent, as though he were personally accountable for what had been demanded of him, "I swear by Allah, I never saw, never heard of that pasha."

Going into one of the large shops on the ground floor of the building, he asked with the same brusqueness of the man who seemed to be the owner, "What happened to Silahtar Omer Pasha's Almshouse?"

The man called to someone who was sitting at a desk inside a glass partition in the shop, "They're looking for Omer Pasha's Whatyoucallit. You know anything about it?"

The other echoed back from the glass compartment, "Omer Pasha's Whatyoucallit. . . Once upon a time I heard tell something about that. It's been nigh onto ten years."

My friend let his arms fall to his sides in hopelessness. Unable to endure hearing the conclusion of what the man was saying, he said, "Come on, let's go!"

After having invited me here repeatedly over the years to show me the monuments and historical structures, he now looked ashamed of the predicament into which he had fallen.

To sooth my friend I said, "That's enough for today. We're both tired. If you like, we can go sightseeing again some more tomorrow."

After having inspected me from under his brooding eyebrows to see if I were making fun of him, he said, "No, no, what have we seen anyhow? You can't go without seeing the Spiral Mosque."

We got into the car, "Do you know the Spiral Mosque?" He asked.

I said I didn't know of it.

One couldn't leave there without seeing the Spiral Mosque because it was the most magnificent mosque in the province.

He asked the driver, "You don't know where anything is, so do you know the Spiral Mosque?"

The driver said, "I know, gran'dad."

"If you had said you didn't know that either, then you would have seen what for."

In the hope of having finally found a place that he was looking for and of showing it to me, he relaxed and explained the Spiral Mosque to me on the way. It was called the Spiral Mosque because it had three separate winding stairways inside of the minarets leading up to the balconies and on the outside it was decorated with winding raised reliefs. The muezzins who climbed the winding stairways of the minarets couldn't see one another but the importance of this mosque lay not in the spiral form of its minarets but in the marble carvings of the squares on the facade. These marble carvings were one of the most beautiful masterpieces of Selchuk architecture, and experts had come all the way from Europe and America to study these marble carvings. These marble carvings were an amazing thing, as fine as lace embroidered by women. One could never gaze one's fill at them.

Just as he was saying, "Now y'll see for yourself," the driver stopped the car.

"Here we be, gran'dad," he said.

Before getting out of the car, my friend, asked, "Where have we got to?"

"You said the Spiral Mosque, gran'dad?"

"Damn it, where's the Mosque? What happened to the Mosque?"

"Oh, the Mosque? The Mosque is behind those buildings yonder. Them are apartments, them over yonder are offices, over there are cloth workshops. . . "

We got out of the car. By persistent searching, we found our way to the Spiral Mosque through the openings. Anyway, the Mosque was still standing. Moved by the joy of having found at least one place we had been looking for, my friend was still singing the praises of the marble carvings of the facade. But when he arrived at the entrance of the Mosque, he broke off his speech and stood there petrified. He stood there for a moment. I was afraid that something would happen to my poor friend but when I tried to take him by the arm, he pushed my hand away violently. He grabbed, at random, one of the men who was going into the Mosque, by the hand. The man must have just have performed his ritual washing because he was rolling his shirt sleeves back down again.

"What happened to the marble carving on this gate?" he asked abruptly, waving with his hand towards the place where the carvings should have been.

Where he pointed, there was no marble to be seen because all the decorations of the gate and the marble of the facade had been painted over, just as they were, with a loud green color called "*hajji* green" and since it had been painted coat over coat, the marble was concealed by the paint.

This time, my friend didn't make a sound. His face was ashen grey. He seemed to be as embarrassed as though he had done all this himself. He climbed back into the car without saying a word.

"To Zullu Baba's Tomb," he said.

The driver asked, "Where is that, gran'dad?" and when that refined, elderly man announced that it was located in such and such a location belonging to the driver's mother, in such a manner and even using the common word for it, I couldn't keep from laughing out loud. My host was frowning. I was biting my lip to keep from laughing.

Holding back my laughter with difficulty, I said, "It must have been a while since you've been to these parts."

"So 'tis, nigh on fifteen years I haven't wandered the town because of my age."

He explained to the driver where Zullu Baba's Tomb was. We went there. We got out of the car. My friend looked around him, hunted about, asked passers-by and shopkeepers about Zullu Baba's Tomb. Anyhow, someone who knew appeared. Underneath a four story building on a side street there was an opening set in four roughly cut stones and this opening was closed off by an iron grating. On the stone sill in front of the opening were some candle drippings. Some votive rags had been tied to the grating. My friend acted as though he had seen something very sad.

"G'dap there, let's go," he said.

He was very embarrassed but he still opposed my suggestion that we all go home. He was determined to persuade me that he had been telling me the truth when he had harped for so long on how he was going to show me a beautiful monument in the town. I thought he felt that he had deceived me. To tell the truth, if I could have seen not such a very beautiful monument but even a middlingly nice looking one, I would have been ready to act enchanted, just to please my friend.

He said to the driver, "Let's go to the Güreniz Cistern."

As usual, the driver didn't know where that was either, but he didn't dare to ask where it was for fear of hearing that part of his mother's anatomy given as the address. Of his own free will, my friend told the driver how to get there. On the way, he explained the Gureniz Cistern to me. It was a cistern from Byzantine times that carried water underground, through vaulted canals, all the way to the town's fortress.

"You'll be amazed when you see it. It's built on numberless marble columns, its inside is very cool and the water in there never dries up."

And when we went to the place he had been talking about, we really were amazed because just as there wasn't anybody who knew where the Güreniz Cistern was, in the place where the cistern should have been there was a huge, eight-story building with a pizza parlor, a pin-ball machine arcade and a night club on the ground floor.

He fiercely refused my request to go home. He had to show me a monumental AND historical building before he could rest. Just to make him happy, I was even looking around trying to find an old building in a town which I didn't know and where I myself had never been before. Oh, if I could only find such a building. . .

Though we hunted with the car for nearly an hour for the Karabay Bridge with its three sections, we could find neither the bridge nor the stream it had been built across.

My friend was getting madder and madder.

"Take us to the Ebenes Monastery," he said.

On the way there he explained the Ebenes Monastery. In this monastery the remains of four or five civilizations could be seen, one on top of the other. There were remains from every civilization, starting all the way back to the Hittites through the Persians, the Romans, the Byzantines and down to the Selchuks but the most valuable thing there was the Byzantine mosaics.

I was gripped by inexpressible feelings, fearing that we wouldn't find the monastery and my friend's feelings would be hurt once again and, yes, what I feared came to pass. There was nothing but an empty space where the monastery should have been.

I couldn't keep myself from laughing at his asking whoever he ran across, "Where's the monastery? What'd you do with the monastery?" and their surprised expressions. No matter how much I tried to hide my laughter, he saw it and was secretly getting mad at me too. But because I was his guest, he couldn't say anything to me.

When he said, "Let's go to the baths," I burst out laughing. I though that he was proposing we go to the baths to wash and relax after such a tiring day.

"Thanks but I don't need a bath," I said.

"Nay, not to take a bath." (He said 'nay', with the old pronunciation.) 'Yonder is an Ottoman bath. Tis worth seeing.' "

He explained while we were on our way to the baths: the baths had one big dome that rested on three smaller domes, they had a cooling room, two hot rooms, and two sweat rooms. The sweat rooms were paved with red, black and white marble. There was a grove of quince trees in front of the baths. The baths were built of cut stone.

We came to the Baths of the Quince Tree. I shouldn't say we came to the baths, we came to where the baths had been. There wasn't even anyone who knew about the baths. My friend fearlessly kept asking all and sundry, "Where are the Baths of the Quince Tree? What the devil did you do with the

Baths of the Quince Tree? What the devil did you do with the great big bathhouse?"

When I insisted that we go back, he persisted out of stubbornness, that we go to see another historic sight.

"Come on there, let's go see the castle moat," he said.

The town's castle and its moat were his last hope. They couldn't have razed the immense castle surely. . . I too hoped that we would be able to see the castle and its moat.

Again, as usual, he explained the place we were going to visit as we were going along in the car:

"The moat that surrounds the castle is one thousand three hundred feet long. The width of the moat is forty yards and the depth is three yards and it is hewed out of solid stone and it's the only moat in the whole world that's hewed out of stone. They filled the moat with water so the enemy couldn't get inside. The castle moat. . . "

Ah, here was where all hell broke loose. As soon as he got out of the car, my aged friend started to yell at the top of his lungs, "God damn it aaall! What have you folks done with the castle moat? What did you do to the moat?"

They had filled the moat in and turned it into a market place. The market place was full to the bursting with sellers, buyers and people carrying things. Baskets, crates, market stands, push carts, stands on wheels, ugly shacks, bags, tin cans, vegetables, greenery . . . the shouts and cries of the market people . . . the ground was all mud. My friend grabbed everybody that came within his grasp by the hand or by the collar, man or woman, buyer or seller, and asked them, "What the devil did y'do with the castle moat?"

The people asked, turned the question back to him in amazement, "What did y'say, mister? What moat? Whose moat? W'happened to the moat?"

Lunch time was long passed. By now my friend's last hope was gone but he didn't want to fall in defeat. He wanted to show me an historic place no matter what and so justify the things he had been telling me all this long time.

As his last hope, he said, "Well, let's go to the Sovanlı Mosque and then go home."

We got into the car and my friend started to explain again. This Sovanlı Mosque that we were about to see didn't have any particular artistic value. The true value of this mosque lay in its privy. It had a privy that was unique in the whole world. The famous German architect and urban planner Jansen had come and seen it and even he was amazed. When he saw it, he took the mayor's hand and said, don't y'all mess this up, y'hear? The architectural value of this privy lay in the fact that the Ottomans created such a ventilation system that no privy smell drifted outside. Jansen just clean lost his head over it. . . You went down to the privies by a stairway of forty stairs from the courtyard of the Mosque. (While my friend was explaining all this, I had all I could do to keep from laughing while I thought of a man needing to go in a hurry and, unable to hold himself for forty stairs, soiling himself before he got there.) After you had gone down those forty stairs, they said there was a road at the bottom. He himself hadn't seen it but they said that a man on horseback could ride down it. Jansen was so utterly amazed at how downright smart the Ottomans had been to find a way to get rid of privy smell that he drew a plan to show when he got back yonder to Germany to say "just see what all these foreigners have got."

I was happy too that we would go home after seeing the Sovanli Mosque. As soon as we stepped into the courtyard, we were assailed by a keen, unbearable odor of urine. People sat around the fountain in the middle of the courtyard, yawning, stretching, sunning themselves. My dear old friend turned this way and that in the courtyard and when he couldn't find what he was looking for, he shouted with all his might, raising his head to the skies, "Damn, where is the privy?"

A helpful person showed us the open door to the privies at the end of the courtyard. They had tacked up over the door to the privies bits of cardboard with "Number one: 100 liras" and "Big number: 150 liras" scrawled on them and in the door to the privies they had lined up a bunch of rusty tin food cans set on a board on top of rusty tin buckets full of water.

My friend turned pale. I was afraid he might have a heart attack. Shoving a man, who was performing his ritual washing with murmured prayers at a water tap, by the nape of the neck, he shouted, "Where is the Privy of the Forty Stairs? Wheere?"

The man turned his head back and looked at him and then, shaking his head from side to side, went back to his ablutions.

Then my friend latched onto a man, walking along with wooden clogs on his bare feet.

"What did you do with the Privy of the Forty Stairs? What'd you do?

I was holding my sides and I thought I would die from laughing. My eyes watered from laughter. So that my friend wouldn't see me laughing, I turned my back and walked a little way away from him. He was still asking everybody he encountered, "What the devil did you do with the Privy of the Forty Stairs?" and they were looking at him stupidly, not understanding a word of what he was saying.

Now he had lost his last hope. The flush in his nose faded and the anger in his eyes diminished and he came over to me.

"C'mon, let's go get some baklava. There's no baklava anywhere like our baklava here," he said.

I almost rolled on the ground with laughter. I held onto the wall. I had a laughing fit.

We got into the car. Neither of us talked. If I had tried to talk, I knew that I would have started laughing again.

It was evening when we got back to the house. When we reached the house, my dear old friend said, "Let's have some raki and hors d'oeuvres."

We sat down to the hors d'oeuvres and raki. I won't attempt to list all the appetizers but I must tell about the baklava. Allah, Allah, so there existed baklava like that? All this time I had been eating baklava that was served me and thinking it was really baklava, whereas I had been eating something that even know the difference. That night I ate more baklava than all the baklava I had ever eaten in my whole life.

I was supposed to stay in that town for three more days. According to my friend's plan, we were supposed to have toured all the historic monuments. Since we had given up on this tour, what could I do for the remaining three days? I ate baklava for three days. When I left, I took three boxes of baklava with me.

My dear old friend said, as he was seeing me off, "Come on now, did you ever eat any baklava like our baklava here?"

"I swear I never have," I said. "It's worth coming here just to eat the baklava."

I weighed myself when I got back to Istanbul. I had gained four and a half kilos in the three days I had been eating the baklava. If I get an opportunity in the near future, I will go back to that South-Eastern town to be a guest of my friend and to eat that historic baklava.

Gaziantep January 9, 1988
[Note: A town whose baklava is famous throughout Turkey]

Aziz Nesin Selected Bibliography

Short Story Collections:

Geriye Kalan [Whatever Remains] 1948
İt Kuyruğu [The Tail of the Dog] 1955
Yedek Parça [Spare Parts] 1955
Fil Hamdi [Hamdi the Elephant] 1955
Damda Deli Var [There's a Madman up on the Roof] 1956
Koltuk [The Armchair] 1957
Kazan Töreni [The Ceremony of the Cauldron] 1957
Toros Canavarı [The Monster of the Taurus Mountains] 1957
Deliler Boşandı [The Madmen have Broken Loose] 1957
Mahallenin Kısmeti [Fate of the Neighborhood] 1957
Ölmüş Eşek [The Dead Donkey] 1957
Hangi Parti Kazanacak? [What Party will Win?] 1957
Havadan Sudan [About This and That] 1957
Bay Düdük [Mister Whistle] 1958
Nazik Alet [The Delicate Instrument] 1958
Gıdıgıdı [Tickle-tickle] 1958
Aferin [Bravo] 1959
Kördüğümü [The Complete Mixup] 1959
Mahmut ile Nigar [Mahmut and Nigar] 1959
Gözüne Gözlük [A Pair of Glasses] 1959
Ah Biz Eşekler [Ah, We Donkeys] 1961

Yüz Liraya bir Deli [A Madman for One Hundred Liras] 1961
Bir Koltuk nasıl Devrilir [How to upset an Armchair (i.e., How
   to Throw a Dignitary out of his Office)] 1961
Biz Adam olmayız [We will Never Amount to Anything] 1961
Sosyalizm geliyor Savulun [Here comes Socialism, Clear the
   Way!] 1965
İhtilali Nasıl yaptık [How we made the Revolution] 1965
Rıfat Bey neden kaşınıyor [Why does Rıfat Bey Scratch?] 1965
Yeşil Renkli Namus Gazı [The Green Gauze of Honor] 1965
Bülbül Yuvası Evler ["Nightingale Nest" Housing Complex]
   1968
Vatan Sağolsun [Long Live the Fatherland (or, It's a Great
   Country but...)] 1968
Yaşasın Memleket [Long live the Country] 1969
İnsanlar Uyanıyor [People are Waking Up] 1972
Büyük Grev [The Big Strike] 1978

Novels:

Kadın olan Erkek [The Man who was a Woman] 1955
Gol Kralı Sait Hopsait [Sait Hopsait, the Goal King] 1957
Erkek Sabahat [Sabahat (a woman's name) the Man] 1957
Nutuk Makinası [The Speechmaking Machine] 1958
Az Gittik Uz Gittik [On and On We Went] 1959
Saçkıran [Iron Breaker] 1959
Zübük [(A name)] 1961
Şimdiki Çocuklar Harika [The Kids Nowadays are Remark-
   able] 1967
Merhaba [Greetings] 1971
Tatlı Betüş [Sweet Betüş] 1974
Ahmet Saves the Day [anthology] 1975
Surname [The Book of Festivals] 1976
Tek Yol [The Only Way] 1978
Kalpazanlık bile Yapılamıyor [They Can't Even Forge Money]
   1984
Yetmiş Yaşım Merhaba [Hail My Seventieth Year] 1984

Maçinli Kíz için Ev [A House for the Girl from Neverneverland] 1987

Nah Kalkíníriz [Hey Lookit, We're Progressing] 1988

Interviews:

Soruşturmalarda [Interviews] 1986

Memoirs:

Bir Sürgünün Hatiralari [The Memoirs of an Exile] 1957

Poliste [In the Hands of the Police] 1967

Aziz Nesin Paris'te [Aziz Nesin in Paris] 1973

Böyle Gelmiş Böyle Gitmez [That's the Way It Always Was but That's Not the Way that It Will Always Be] part one, 1966, part two, 1976 [Translated as Istanbul Boy] 1977, 1979

Plays:

Biraz Gelirmisiniz? [Would You Please Come Here for a Little While?] 1958

Bir şey yap, Met [Do Something, Met] 1959

Düdükçülerle Fırçaçıların Savaşı [The War of the Whistle Makers and the Brush Makers] 1968

Üç Karagöz Oyunu [Three Shadow Plays] 1968

Çiçu, 1970

Legendary and fantastic stories:

Memleketin birinde [In a certain country] 1958

Hoptirinam [Hoopla] 1960

Tut Elimden Rovni [Hold my Hand, Rovni] 1970

Hadi Öldürsene Canikom [Go on and Kill me, Sweety] 1970

Uyusana Tosunum [Sleep Tight, my Darling Boy] 1971

Yaşar ne Yaşar ne Yaşamaz [Yasar ("The Living One") is Neither Dead nor Alive] 1977

Beş kisa Oyun [Five Short Plays] 1979

Unpublished Plays:

Barbaros'un Torunu [The Grandson of Barbarossa]
Hakkımı ver Hakkı [Give Me My Rights, Hakki (a man's name
meaning "Righteous")]

Folk Tales:

Aziz Dededen Masallar [Tales from Grandfather Aziz] n.d.

Satire:

Azizname [The Book of Aziz] 1970

Travel Diaries:

Duyduk Duymadık Demeyin [Don't Say that You Haven't
Heard (the Sultan's Proclamation)] 1976
Dünya Kazan Ben Kepçe [I've Combed the World with a Fine-
Toothed Comb] 1977
Nesin is Editor and Publisher of Nesin Vakfı Edebiyat Yıllığı
[Nesin Foundation Literary Year Book] 1976-